american sign language DeMYSTiFieD

Kristin Mulrooney, Ph.D.

Mc Graw Hill

New York Chicago San Francisco Lisbon London Madrid Mexico City
Milan New Delhi San Juan Seoul Singapore Sydney Toronto

1 2 3 4 5 6 7 8 9 10 11 12 13 14 15   WFR/WFR   0 9

ISBN   978-0-07-160137-5 (book and DVD)
MHID   0-07-160137-6 (book and DVD)

ISBN   978-0-07-160140-5 (book)
MHID   0-07-160140-6 (book)
Library of Congress Control Number 200843479

DVD design, production, and direction by Patrick Harris of Patrick Harris Digital.
DVD script by Kristin Mulrooney.
DVD ASL model: Flavia Fleischer.
Interior screen shots by Patrick Harris of Patrick Harris Digital.

McGraw-Hill books are available at special quantity discounts to use as premiums and
sales promotions or for use in corporate training programs. To contact a representative,
please e-mail us at bulksales@mcgraw-hill.com.

This book is dedicated to the memory of Dr. Lawrence Fleischer, whose work has inspired many people. It is our responsibility to continue his efforts to educate people about ASL and the Deaf community. May we do so with as much passion and dedication as he.

CONTENTS

Introduction   vii

CHAPTER 1   **About American Sign Language**   1

CHAPTER 2   **Body Language and Facial Expressions**   16

CHAPTER 3   **Grammar and Sentence Structure**   32

CHAPTER 4   **Verbs**   62

CHAPTER 5   **Deaf Etiquette**   85

CHAPTER 6   **Variation in ASL**   99

CHAPTER 7   **Meeting, Greeting, and Good-Byes**   113

CHAPTER 8   **Asking Questions**   135

CHAPTER 9   **Describing People and Things**   153

CHAPTER 10   **Expressing Likes and Dislikes**   170

CHAPTER 11   **Expressing Past, Present, and Future**   187

CHAPTER 12   **The Manual Alphabet: Finger Spelling**   203

CHAPTER 13   **Numbers, Dates, and Time**   215

CHAPTER 14   **Family and Friends**   241

CHAPTER 15   **Health**   259

             Appendix: Glossing Conventions   285
             Answer Key to Chapter Quizzes   288
             Index   291

INTRODUCTION

American Sign Language Demystified is just one in a series of products that offers comprehensive instruction to an independent learner or classroom student. You chose this book and DVD package because you are thinking about studying American Sign Language (ASL) and need a clear, uncomplicated approach.

Perhaps you've already learned another language besides the one you grew up with, but ASL is different from any language you may know. The visual aspect—delivered through hand(s), facial expression, body movement, and spatial dimension—makes it unique. Welcome to the rich experience of ASL! Here you will learn its history, key vocabulary and grammar, etiquette, and lots more.

How to Use This Book and DVD

The book has fifteen chapters total, each with a summary of concepts learned and a quiz to test your retention. You can read the chapters sequentially and do all the oral and written practices to reinforce the material presented, or depending on your experience and skill level, you can jump from part to part as needed.

The answers for the chapter quizzes can be found in the answer key.

Each chapter is organized by topics, making it easy to digest information in small capsules. Spend one week with each chapter, taking one to two hours each day to absorb and practice the material. Try not to rush—go at a steady pace. And don't get discouraged. Learning a new language is difficult and takes time and concentration, but I hope that the organization of this book and DVD will make the effort less demanding.

Because ASL is a visual language, the DVD is more than an adjunct to the book—it is an essential part of the learning process. The "screen grabs" in the book are not meant to fully illustrate a sign sequence or phrase; rather, they are meant to function as visual references to what's shown on the DVD. The DVD contains all the signs

and phrases in the book as well as additional vocabulary, and you will study the DVD in order to replicate the signs. In addition, the DVD contains added vocabulary chapters not found in the book. Chapter 16 on the DVD covers travel vocabulary, Chapter 17 includes vocabulary related to food, Chapter 18 covers shopping, Chapter 19 covers technology of all kinds (computer, deaf-related, media, and more), and Chapter 20 includes a wide range of additional terms that the begnning ASL student will want to master.

A word in one language may not have a corresponding word in another, and this is true of ASL and English. In this book, ASL signs are represented by English words written in all capital letters. The translations, or *glosses*, appear either in the text or in a caption. Information on how to understand the glosses is given in Chapter 1 as well as in the Appendix.

CHAPTER 1

About American Sign Language

American Sign Language (ASL) uses all the abilities required by any other language. People who use it are able to express any idea, feeling, thought, or experience they may have. There is no limit to what can be discussed, debated, described, or conveyed. What distinguishes ASL—and what is likely its most fascinating feature—is how the language is transmitted and received. Spoken languages (such as French, Spanish, or English) produce words through the actions of the vocal tract, which create sounds that are perceived through audition. ASL, however, produces signs by the actions of the face, hands, and the rest of the body, which are perceived visually. This difference in modality impacts the form of the language but not the function.

As you progress through this book, you will begin to understand how ASL capitalizes on its visual aspects to express meaning. To give you a preview, think about how you have two hands but only one tongue. You can utter only one word at a time because you have one tongue with which to articulate the sounds necessary to utter a word. ASL signers can, and often do, produce two different signs simultaneously, one with each hand.

Deaf and hard-of-hearing people in the United States and parts of Canada use ASL as their primary language for face-to-face communication. It developed independently of English and is not a representation of spoken English. It is impossible to produce grammatically correct ASL and speak grammatically correct English at the same time. This would be similar to attempting to speak English and simultaneously write the same words in Spanish. While there are some similarities between the languages—for example, both English and ASL share the same basic word order (subject-verb-object)—there are more differences. These differences include ASL's use of facial expressions to express grammatical information, use of depicting and indicating verbs, use of space, and so on. All languages can express the same concepts, but they do so with different forms and grammatical structures. Suppose someone was gazing at the Colorado River rushing through the Grand Canyon. An English speaker might describe it as "a large river." A Spanish speaker, however, would say, "*un río grande.*" Both languages are describing the idea that it is a large body of water, but placement of the adjective before or after the noun varies. You will have a much easier time learning ASL (or any foreign language, for that matter) once you start learning how it expresses the same *concept* from your language rather than the same grammatical structure.

The History of ASL

Sign languages exist because not all humans can hear. The fact that a spoken language is not accessible to deaf people makes it virtually impossible to learn and use. Deaf people adapted their language to circumvent the need to use their voices and ears and replaced the auditory mode with the visual one. The use of a visual language is not unique to Deaf people. In America, the Great Plains Indians developed a system of signing that was used for intertribal communication. While these communications were codes rather than language, the use of a visual language rather than a spoken one remains significant.

What is now called "American Sign Language" can be traced back to 1817 to the founding of the nation's first school for deaf people in Hartford, Connecticut. The opening of this school brought together a number of factors that contributed to the development of ASL. The first was the desire to educate Deaf children in the United States. A man by the name of Thomas Hopkins Gallaudet met a young Deaf girl, Alice Cogswell, and after observing and interacting with her, he believed she could and should receive an education. Alice's father, Dr. Mason Fitch Cogswell, was equally committed to this idea and worked with other prominent citizens to raise funds to send the eager Gallaudet to Europe to study methods of teaching the deaf.

Gallaudet initially went to a school for the deaf in London that was operated by the Braidwood family, who denied training to prospective teachers unless they agreed to pay the family for each deaf child who would be educated using their methods. Gallaudet refused this requirement or to accept the tenets of the Braidwood system. After thirteen months in London, he believed he would be unable to learn how to teach deaf children and would have to return to the United States.

As it happened, the director of the French Institute for the Deaf in Paris, Abbé Sicard, was in London at the same time as Gallaudet. Sicard and his two deaf assistants, Jean Massieu and Laurent Clerc, gave lectures and demonstrated the methods they used to teach deaf children in France. After attending a lecture, Gallaudet met with Sicard and his assistants and accepted their invitation to enter the teacher preparation program at the French school.

Laurent Clerc guided Gallaudet's training, but their time together was abbreviated because of Gallaudet's limited funds. He was forced to return to the United States before mastering all the techniques and manual communication skills he was studying. He convinced Sicard to allow Clerc to come to America and help him establish a school that would employ the methods used by the French. Sicard and Clerc both agreed, and on the fifty-five-day ocean voyage, Gallaudet continued to learn sign language from Clerc, while Clerc learned English from him.

Gallaudet and Clerc opened the American School for the Deaf on April 15, 1817. They relied on a visual communication method to instruct the children who attended. The desire to teach deaf children led to the second significant factor in the development of what would later be ASL: a community of users. Prior to this, deaf children had been isolated from one another throughout the United States. The Congregational Church of New England estimated that there were eighty deaf children in New England and approximately eight hundred in the entire country. These children had little, if any, contact with other deaf people.

There were exceptions. In Henniker, New Hampshire, there was a community that used signing to communicate. Another was found on the isolated island of Martha's Vineyard off the coast of Massachusetts. Early Vineyard settlers carried a gene for deafness, and over the years, marriage within this limited population resulted in each subsequent generation having a greater number of deaf people. By the mid-nineteenth century, one out of four babies born in the village of Chilmark was deaf. It is believed that the first deaf person to arrive on Martha's Vineyard, Jonathan Lambert, used a sign language that was probably related to one of the Kentish dialects of British Sign Language. As the deaf population grew, the use of sign language also grew and became known as Martha's Vineyard Sign Language (MVSL). MVSL was unique because both hearing and deaf people used it. Due to the large proportion of deaf people in the population, government business was routinely conducted using MVSL to ensure that everyone was able to participate.

Ironically, it was the establishment of the American School for the Deaf that contributed to the decline of the deaf population on Martha's Vineyard and the eventual demise of MVSL. Once the school opened, children from the Vineyard began to attend. They did not return to the island after graduation, opting to remain on the mainland because of better economic opportunities. The last deaf Vineyard native passed away in the 1950s.

As stated before, the school brought together many different forms of signing for the first time. The Vineyard students had a native sign language. Clerc brought his knowledge and use of French Sign Language to the school. It is also likely that other students, especially those with deaf siblings, had created their own "home-signing" systems to communicate. The interaction of all these people and languages resulted in the early version of ASL.

A third significant factor in the history of ASL grew out of the first two: educated deaf people who shared a native sign language. The graduates of the American School for the Deaf migrated to other areas of the country and established new schools: New York School for the Deaf (1818) and Pennsylvania School for the Deaf (1820). These institutions enabled more deaf children to be educated and exposed them to sign language, which could then continue to flourish. The fact that deaf people were being educated meant that they could be gainfully employed and participate in American society. Further evidence of this highly educated community was the establishment of Gallaudet College (now Gallaudet University) in Washington, D.C., in 1864. Thomas Hopkins Gallaudet's son, Edward Miner Gallaudet—with the help of Amos Kendall—opened the first and only liberal arts college for deaf people in the world.

An event in 1880 not only made one of the biggest impacts on the education of deaf people, but it almost eliminated the use of ASL. This event was an international conference of deaf educators held in Milan. A resolution was passed that banned the use of sign languages to teach deaf children, declaring that oral education (use of speech) was better than manual (sign) education. Thomas Gallaudet, Edward Miner Gallaudet, Issac Peet, James Denison, and Charles Stoddard represented the United States at the conference. They were strongly opposed to the resolution, but their efforts failed to prevent its passage. The repercussions from the Milan conference were immediate and severe. Deaf teachers across the United States lost their jobs. This removed native sign language models from schools, stifling the transmission of the language. The focus of deaf education shifted from teaching students reading, writing, history, and math to teaching them how to speak and lip-read. The basis of the shift was the belief that these skills were more important to a deaf person's success in society than basic literacy skills. ASL, which for more than sixty years had been used and accepted, was suddenly viewed negatively as something to which deaf people should not be exposed.

The education of deaf children from 1880 to the 1960s was dominated by the oral approach, and many involved in educating deaf children worked to eliminate the use of sign language. Despite this, the latter prevailed. The first, and arguably biggest, reason it survived was because there were still deaf people in the United States who knew that a visual language was their most efficient means of face-to-face communication. Second, deaf people continued to marry each other and expose succeeding generations of children to ASL. These children would attend schools for the deaf and teach other students the language when teachers were not around. Third, Edward Miner Gallaudet decided that sign language would continue to be the language of instruction at Gallaudet College. Finally, the highly educated members of the U.S. deaf population in 1880 came together to work actively to preserve their language by creating the National Association for the Deaf (NAD). This was the first nationwide citizens' association in the country dedicated to maintaining ASL and preserving the rights of deaf people. Despite all efforts to the contrary, deaf people continued to use and teach ASL to subsequent generations.

The fact that Gallaudet College continued to use sign language proved to be vital in ASL's eventual revitalization. In 1955, William C. Stokoe was hired to teach English at Gallaudet. He arrived at the college not knowing any sign language. After a short while of observing students signing, he began to suggest to his colleagues that signing was a distinct linguistic system. This idea was dismissed, and he was told time and again that signing simply mimicked speech. Stokoe was undeterred and set out to prove that signing was, in fact, a language independent of English.

Over the next five years, Stokoe and two additional researchers—Dorothy Casterline and Carl Croneberg—worked systematically to analyze signs. Stokoe published *Sign Language Structure: An Outline of the Visual Communication Systems of the American Deaf* in 1960. In this monograph he laid out the basis for his assertion that signing was a distinct language. He, Casterline, and Croneberg continued to work together and, in 1965, cowrote *A Dictionary of American Sign Language on Linguistic Principles.* As an example of the analysis, we can look at the analysis of the phonology of a sign. He demonstrated how each individual sign is created from a combination of three features—a handshape, a location, and a movement—and that these combinations of parts parallel how words in spoken languages can be broken down into component parts.

The impact of Stokoe's research was immediate and dramatic. He not only revolutionized how educators viewed sign language, now referred to as ASL, but he altered how linguists viewed language in general. Until his work was published, *language* was synonymous with *speech*. Stokoe convincingly proved that this was not accurate and that the form of a language is variable; it can be spoken or signed. The capacity to transmit meaningful utterances is independent of modality. Sign languages have developed to take advantage of the resources available to the body and eyes. Additionally, Stokoe's work changed the way deaf people viewed their own language. He justified what they had known intuitively for more than one hundred years—that they had a full-fledged language distinct from English.

From 1965 to the present, the field of sign language linguistics has exploded. There have been advances to most aspects of the theories Stokoe presented. This book reflects the most recent theories of the linguistic structure of ASL. What you will likely realize is how complex a language it is. People often say, "Learning ASL must be easy because you just need to learn some signs for English words, and the signs are so simple!" This is a misconception I hope to put to rest once and for all, but in a way that doesn't deter you from pursuing your desire to learn this language.

Writing ASL

American English is the dialect of English spoken in the United States. It is distinct from the British English that is spoken in the United Kingdom. Since the two dialects are related, U.S. travelers do not encounter much difficulty conversing with speakers of British English. However, there are differences that often cause speakers of the two dialects to pause. For instance, an American may be able to figure out that *fizzy drink* refers to a soft drink, but a word like *bonnet* could cause confusion (the American thinks it means something worn on the head when the British speaker refers to the hood of a car). In addition to lexical differences, there are also phonological differences, such as how vowels are pronounced. The two dialects do, however, share a system to record the spoken language: the writing system.

A written language is the representation of a spoken language. Different systems are used to represent spoken languages: consonant alphabets (Arabic), phonemic alphabets (Greek), syllabic alphabets (Burmese), syllabaries (Japanese), logographic (Chinese). The differences in the systems are rooted in what they attempt to represent. Each symbol in a phonemic alphabets represent one or more phonemes (sounds). Logographic systems use symbols that represent a word, morpheme, or semantic unit, with the shape of the symbol often resembling the thing it represents. All written systems are invented and must be learned. The written system I am using to write these words is an example of how English speakers have agreed to represent their spoken language. Ask any elementary school children and they will tell you how frustrating the system can be. We agreed, for example, to represent the three sounds / h /, / æ /, and / v / as *have* with four written symbols *h*, *a*, *v*, and *e*. And how about a word like *psychology*?

The point is that written systems are artificial systems for documenting the spoken form of languages, and the two are distinct from one another. It is common for a person to be able to speak a language without knowing how to write or read it. Often one written system is used to represent two different spoken systems (Mandarin Chinese and Cantonese Chinese, for instance). There are, in fact, far fewer writing systems representing languages than there are spoken languages in the world. Although there are approximately sixty-eight hundred known spoken languages, there are only about two hundred written systems. It is far more common for languages not to have a written system.

ASL is among the many languages that does not have a written form. Stokoe introduced a system for writing signs, and people—primarily linguists—often use the Stokoe Notation System as a way of representing signs. You will learn more about this system in Chapter 3. In recent years, attempts have been made to develop a writing system for sign languages that could be used by anyone. The most widely used is SignWriting developed by Valerie Sutton in 1974 (see signwriting.org for examples).

Despite these attempts, one system has not been accepted for use in the Deaf community. The reason for this is likely because written systems are not effective in capturing the linguistic features unique to a visual language—facial expressions, use of space, and multiple articulators, to name a few. Although written systems are useful in preserving a language, they are only effective if they can do so efficiently and accurately. To date, no such system exists for ASL. It is important to point out that many ASL users read and write English. Deaf communities throughout history have acknowledged the importance of learning the written language of the majority in their country.

How then do people preserve sign language? One way, which is common to many languages that do not have a written system, is the existence of a strong storytelling tradition. The Deaf community in America highly values skilled storytellers who pass along narratives, jokes, and poems from one generation to the next.

Also, advancing technology allowed for ASL to be filmed starting in the early 1900s. Thirty-three years after the NAD was established and began to move toward preserving ASL against eradication, Deaf people began to use film to record people signing. The oldest of these films, recorded by the NAD, are from 1913. In the most famous, titled *Preservation of the Sign Language*, then-president of the NAD, George W. Veditz, passionately argues about the importance of preserving the sign language.

GLOSSING CONVENTIONS

Over time, people have relied on the use of *glosses*—English words used to represent signs. A gloss is written in all capital letters to distinguish it from the written English word. For example, the sign below would be glossed as WITH.

WITH

Glossing ASL is often difficult because there is no single English word that is equivalent to an ASL sign, as shown here:

BECOME-IMMERSED-IN

This sign means "to become immersed in," as when someone becomes fascinated by a new hobby and spends a large amount of time mastering it. English does not have a single word for this. Any translator or interpreter will tell you this is common when working between two languages. You will often encounter a word or phrase that does not have an equivalent in the other language. When this occurs with ASL, two or more English words are used with hyphens between them to represent the sign.

Some signs are actually made up of two individual signs that have become a compound. An example is a sign glossed as TRUE^BUSINESS, which is illustrated here:

TRUE^BUSINESS

This is used when a signer wants to emphasize what actually happened in a given situation.

Glosses are useful in that they provide a means of documenting ASL using text. They therefore provide a means of writing down what a person sees. However, there are some disadvantages as well. One is that glosses do not capture everything necessary to understand the meaning of an ASL sign. Facial expressions, eyes, where a sign is directed in space, and body position are not captured in a gloss. Second, because English may not have an equivalent term, you are left using something that is "close" but not transparent enough for many people to figure out the sign. Finally, glosses are used to label lexical signs; however, the meaning is sometimes conveyed through the use of a gesture or facial expression. This information is omitted if you are only recording what your hands produce. Take, for example, the expressions produced here:

The signer in both examples effectively conveys information to her interlocutor. In the first photo, she demonstrates her surprise, and in the second, she demonstrates the fact that she doesn't know something. Neither example uses an ASL sign to transmit the information. If we only wrote down a gloss for what was produced by the hands, this information would be omitted.

In this book I will be using glosses to talk about different ASL signs. I want to review some of the conventions I will use so you are better able to "read" the glosses.

To identify signs:

1. A single capitalized English word is used to identify a single ASL sign:

HOUSE

2. Capitalized English words separated by hyphens represent a single ASL sign:

OH-I-SEE

3. Two capitalized English words connected by a ^ symbol indicate that two ASL signs have been combined into a single sign:

TRUE^BUSINESS

4. Capitalized letters separated by hyphens represent a sequence of alphabetic character signs used to spell a word:

S-H-E-L-F

5. A capitalized English word that begins with a # symbol represents a lexical ASL sign that originally began as a sequence of alphabetic character signs:

#JOB

6. PRO-1 is used to represent a first person singular pronoun. ASL does not have separate signs meaning "me" and "I" as English does:

PRO-1

7. Two capitalized English words within brackets represent two bound ASL morphemes:

{FOUR}{O'CLOCK}

8. A capitalized English word with a grammatical process in brackets next to it, which represents a difference in how the sign is articulated, adding meaning to the sign:

STUDY[CONTINUATIVE]

9. When a sequence of glosses is accompanied by a nonmanual signal that provides specific grammatical information, a line is written over the glosses, which are followed by a symbol indicating the nonmanual sign that was expressed:

neg
‾‾‾‾‾‾‾‾‾‾‾‾‾‾‾‾‾‾‾‾‾‾‾‾‾‾‾
PRO-1 UNDERSTAND/ I don't understand.

10. When a gesture is used, its meaning within the specific context is placed in quotation marks:

"don't know"

11. If a signer uses both hands at the same time to produce two different signs, the glosses are written on top of each other, the top line referring to the strong hand and the bottom line to the weak hand:

BOY
GIRL

Many signs in ASL can be directed in space. This means you can move them in different directions when you sign. How you move them provides additional information about the subject and object. I will introduce additional notation conventions used to write down these signs later. I will also provide translations of signs or sequences of signs in English with quotation marks around them to set them off from the text.

Sign Languages Around the World

One of the most common misconceptions people who are not familiar with ASL have is the belief that it is the universal language of deaf people all over the world. Stokoe named the communication system he studied "American" Sign Language because he realized that each country would have its own sign language, independent of the majority of its spoken language(s) and different from sign languages in other countries. This is, indeed, the case.

Some spoken languages are similar to others (English, for instance, is derived from German and therefore still retains influences from its Germanic ancestry). Of course, it has changed significantly over time, and someone who is a native English speaker will not be able to converse with a native German speaker without first studying German. Sign languages follow the same pattern. ASL, for example, has a connection to French Sign Language (*langue des signes française*, or LSF) and the languages share some features. ASL has some cognates—signs that are identical or very similar to LSF. The languages have diverged significantly, however, since the time of Gallaudet and Clerc, and an ASL signer would need to study LSF prior to having a meaningful conversation.

Deaf people may have an advantage over people who use spoken languages when it comes to interacting with deaf people from other countries. Deaf people in the United States interact frequently with speakers of English. Because of this, they have developed strategies for communicating with people who don't know ASL. They may gesture, use exaggerated facial expressions, or write short notes. When traveling abroad, they can employ many of these communication techniques with deaf people who use different sign languages. It may be possible for an LSF user and an ASL user to convey simple information to, or get it from, one another through basic communication strategies, but to have a discussion about complex concepts or issues through gestures alone would be impossible.

Other Sign Communication Systems

This book introduces you to ASL, a language that developed naturally from a community of deaf people. As previously stated, this language is distinct from English and has many linguistic features that English does not have. A number of artificial communication systems have been created—primarily for use in educational settings—that use signs to manually code spoken English. These systems include Signing Exact English 1, Signing Exact English 2, Linguistics of Visual English, and cued speech. The goal of these systems is to use signs to visually represent English. Each system has its own particular set of rules for accomplishing this, but the basic idea is to manually produce everything that would be said in English. This means including signs for prefixes, suffixes, and verb markers; distinguishing between verb forms (*have* versus *has*); and following the syntactic structure of English. As a result, it takes many more manual signs to produce the same sentence using these systems than using ASL. It is imperative to point out that these are artificial communication systems and are not to be substituted for signed languages.

Another sign communication system that is sometimes used is when people speak English while they are signing. This is called simultaneous communication, or Sim-Com. This system arose from the idea that it would allow deaf people to see spoken English via the lips and manual signs. In addition, some hard-of-hearing people would be able to hear some of the words. However, the effectiveness of Sim-Com is marginal. The difficulty lies in the fact that it is impossible to speak grammatically correct English and sign grammatically correct ASL at the same time. It would be similar to someone trying to speak grammatically correct English while writing the same sentences in grammatically correct Spanish.

In practice, what happens is the spoken English portion is uttered accurately, although sometimes with a slightly awkward cadence. The sign portion, however, is often compromised, with entire stretches of signs being omitted. For people who can hear, it seems to be effective because they can simply listen to the spoken English, but deaf people often struggle to comprehend the manual portion, which often lacks enough components. Users of Sim-Com do not produce a sign for every word that is spoken. The absence of equivalent manual components makes comprehension impossible.

Many deaf people have been exposed to one or more of these manually coded English systems and are able to use them in addition to ASL when necessary. However, the majority of deaf people feel most comfortable using ASL. You may notice as you learn ASL that deaf people will actually switch to one of the manually coded English systems when interacting with you. This is because they think it is easier for the non-ASL user to understand a code system based on English. This may not be an accurate assumption, but the switch happens nonetheless. Other ASL users will continue to use ASL but choose simpler signs and less complex sentences. This is similar to what English speakers do with people who are learning English. The goal is to simplify the language to ensure better comprehension.

Chapter Summary

In this chapter, you learned the following:

1. That American Sign Language (ASL) is a language that has its own linguistic structure independent from English and other spoken languages.

2. The historical development of ASL from the establishment of the American School for the Deaf in 1817 by Thomas Hopkins Gallaudet and Laurent Clerc to the recognition of it as a language in 1960 by William Stokoe.

3. A method for writing down ASL signs that relies on English glosses.

4. That ASL is not a universal sign language. Rather, each country has its own indigenous sign language independent of its native spoken language and of other sign languages. Each country's sign language may also have its own dialects.

5. That manually coded English communication systems have been developed to represent spoken English. These systems are not languages and are vastly different than ASL.

QUIZ

1. True or false: American Sign Language is a language derived from English.

2. True or false: American Sign language is a universal sign language.

3. True or false: American Sign Language has a written system.

4. True or false: It is possible to speak grammatical English and sign grammatical ASL at the same time.

5. The American School for the Deaf was established in Hartford, Connecticut, in what year?

6. Who first identified ASL as a language?

7. What happened in 1880 that nearly eliminated the use of ASL?

8. What are English glosses?

9. Stokoe demonstrated that every sign is created from a combination of what three things?

10. *A Dictionary of American Sign Language on Linguistic Principles* was published in what year?

CHAPTER 2

Body Language and Facial Expressions

The two comments heard most often from people who are unfamiliar with ASL or just learning ASL are: "ASL signers are so expressive," and "I don't know how to use my body when I'm signing." These statements highlight features of ASL that differ from spoken English: the use of the face and body to convey information. This is not to say that English speakers never use their bodies or faces. They regularly produce facial expressions while speaking, such as widening their eyes and rounding their mouth to express the emotion of surprise. If they are upset their forehead may furrow and their lips turn downward. The difference with ASL is that the face is used to express grammatical information in addition to emotive information. I often tell people studying ASL that learning to use their faces feels similar to learning to produce sounds not in the phonological English system. The rolling r in Spanish, for instance, requires practice and attention, because it is not a sound that a non-native tongue is accustomed to producing.

I also emphasize that you cannot ignore how the face and body are used in ASL and still expect to become a competent user of the language. This is the reason I

16

discuss it in the second chapter of this book. People are easily distracted by memorizing the lexical components of the language (the signs), while dismissing the face and body as secondary. This is a significant misconception. Not studying what the face and body contribute would be like ignoring how to pronounce words correctly or speaking in monotone. If you spoke in a monotone, other English speakers would likely be able to figure out what you were saying, but the exchange would not be smooth and misunderstandings would be frequent.

My objective in this chapter is simply to outline the different ways the face and body are used in ASL. You will receive detailed instructions in subsequent chapters on how to apply this information to specific types of information.

Facial Expressions

Facial expressions can be used to convey grammatical information, emotions, and discursive information. These will be explained in the next few sections.

IDENTIFYING BASIC SENTENCE STRUCTURES

"You are?"

"You are!"

These two English sentences have the same words, but their meanings are different. In the first—"You are?"—I am inquiring as to who you are, most likely what your name is. In the second—"You are!"—I am expressing surprise or excitement about something you have just told me. Perhaps you are a close friend and have informed me that you are moving across the country. The difference in meaning is derived not from the words, but from the intonation in which the sentences are uttered. To produce a question, there is a rising intonation on the word *are*. The intonation for the exclamation is different in that the word *are* is said a bit louder, stressing it more than the word *you*. For speakers of English, these differences are subtle but significant.

ASL relies on facial expressions to make the same distinctions as voice intonation does. For example, the difference between the English statement "You are leaving" and the question "Are you leaving?" is a change in facial expression. Here are the two sentences as they are produced in ASL (for more glossing information regarding verbs, see Chapter 4):

You are leaving.

PRO^{→X} LEAVE

You are leaving?

PRO^{→X} LEAVE?

In the statement PRO^{→X} LEAVE, the signer's face is in what is referred to as a neutral expression. When the signer asks

PRO^{→X} LEAVE?

as a question, however, her eyebrows are raised and her head tilts forward slightly. You can see why selecting and using the correct facial expression is so important in ASL.

ASL has the same four basic sentence structures that English has: declarative, interrogative, imperative, and conditional. In Chapter 3, I will explain in greater detail how to produce these different types of sentences. What is important for you to understand now is that facial expressions are a significant component to producing these sentences grammatically.

GRAMMATICAL ASPECT

The grammatical aspect of a verb defines the temporal flow (or lack thereof) in the described event or state. In English we have the progressive, or continuous, aspect. An example of this would be "I am walking." It is on ongoing event. The second is the perfect, or completed aspect, such as "I have walked." It is also possible to have both: "I have been walking."

Compared to those in some other languages, English verbs express less aspectual information. For instance, in Polish, it is possible for a verb to express a continuous state: *Bede stac* means "I will be standing."

Facial expressions are one component of producing grammatical aspect in ASL. The other component is changing the movement of the verb, which will be explained in Chapter 4. Take the English sentence "I was studying for a long time." In ASL it would be produced like this:

PRO-1 STUDY-FOR-LONG-TIME

Notice the signer's puffed checks, which are made at the same time the sign is articulated. This facial expression is necessary for the grammatical production of this sign. As you continue through the book, it is important that you pay attention to how the face is used. It is often difficult for people learning ASL to become accustomed to using their face to convey grammatical information, but it is critical to becoming a skilled ASL user.

EMOTIVE INFORMATION

The face is used to express emotive information in ASL as it is in English. Signers can convey emotions such as surprise, anger, fear, or joy facially in the same way that speakers can accompany spoken utterances with expressions that parallel the content of their message. The following examples illustrate how facial expressions convey emotive information:

PRO-1 THRILL   **PRO-X MAD**

PRO-1 SHOCK

It is also possible for a signer to simply make a facial expression without an accompanying lexical sign. When this happens, the expression itself is the message. Such "stand-alone" expressions often occur in narratives and are used to convey a character's response or interpretation of an event. The following examples illustrate how a signer is able to use facial expressions without any lexical signs:

DISCURSIVE INFORMATION

When English speakers engage in conversation, the listener often provides the speaker with feedback that he is listening. This feedback can be auditory, such as "Oh yeah," "I know," "Mm," "Really," or "Are you serious?" The listener can also shake his head or nod to further signal to the speaker that he is following what is being said.

People engaged in an ASL conversation do the same thing. One way they can provide feedback signals is by using their face. This is one of the most subtle, and perhaps most foreign, signals to speakers of English. The signer flexes and releases one side of her nose repeatedly. This results in a slight crinkling of the nose, which provides feedback to the signer that the person is attending to and agreeing with what is being signed. Look at the examples on the DVD to see what it looks like in practice.

Eye gaze is another important way the face is used in discourse. This one may seem obvious, but it is worth emphasizing because eye gaze behavior for people using spoken languages is different than that for people using signed languages. Because signed languages are processed visually, whether or not you are looking at the signer is a dramatic signal as to whether or not you are attending to what is being signed. Spoken languages do not have the same constraints. It is possible, and often happens, that the listener does not look at the speaker. Since the language is processed auditorily, you do not have to see the speaker. While a speaker may become annoyed or bothered if a listener never makes eye contact, he still knows his message is being heard without it. Signers do not have this assurance. Eye gaze therefore has significant importance in signed interactions. If the receiver breaks eye contact, the signer knows her message is not being received, so it is important to maintain eye contact with another signer.

Maintaining eye contact is often easier said than done with people learning ASL. In spoken English, looking at a speaker for long stretches is perceived as staring rather than attending and often leaves the speaker and listener uncomfortable. For this reason, listeners will periodically break eye contact with a speaker. The acceptable length of time a person can maintain eye contact with a signer is much longer, because it is necessary for reception of the message. New signers who are unaccustomed to the longer gaze times frequently revert back to the habit of shorter eye contact. This habit is often disconcerting to ASL users because it can be interpreted as boredom or a desire to end the conversation. I cannot give you an exact length of time to watch a signer without changing your eye gaze, but know that breaking eye contact sends a much different message in ASL than in spoken English.

CONVEYING A CHARACTER

The face can also be used to indicate different characters or speakers in discourse. A parallel to this in spoken English would be how people sometimes change their voice to represent a different speaker. For instance, using a lower voice may denote a male speaker, while a high-pitched voice may be used to represent a child. These vocal changes are not mandatory when speakers tell a story, but they can be used to enhance a narrative.

Changes in facial expressions can serve the same purpose in ASL. Suppose a narrator is telling a story about an experience he had in school. At one point in the story, the principal of the school begins to reprimand the narrator (as a child). The narrator may take on a serious facial expression while conveying the principal's side of the exchange, which might look like this:

You can't leave the classroom by yourself!

PRO-X FORBID LEAVE CLASSROOM ALONE

The serious expression gives the impression that the principal is ordering the student to do something, and also that he is the authority and therefore has the right to make such a statement.

Use of the Body

The body is used in different ways to convey information in ASL. The following sections describe how this is done.

PRODUCING SIGNS

I mentioned in Chapter 1 that one difference between how sign languages and spoken languages are produced is that sign languages have more articulators (face, hands, body). Expanding on this point, the articulators in sign languages can interact with each other. One example of this is how the body can be used to produce signs. As you will see in subsequent chapters, the body is an active articulator for many signs. It would be impossible to list them all in this chapter, but here are a few to help you visualize how the body itself is a component of signs:

COP

IMPROVE

BROKE

KNOW

As you can see, the body itself—including the torso, arms, neck, and forehead—is used in the production of the signs. It will become apparent as you continue through the book that the body is often an integral part of grammatical ASL.

INDICATING DIFFERENT SIGNERS

The next two sections describe ways ASL uses the body to express discursive information. The first is distinguishing between signers. This is most often used when conveying what two or more people did or signed.

In spoken English, a person might relay a conversation she had with someone, as illustrated by the following text: "So Jamie says to me, 'I have to use the car tomorrow,' and I respond, 'You do? I thought you didn't need it.' And he replies, 'I didn't think I did, but something has come up.'"

The narrator has several ways to indicate who is speaking in the story. One is using a proper name to identify the speaker, as in "So Jamie says to me." The second is the use of pronouns. In the preceding dialogue, the narrator uses *I* to refer to herself and *he* to refer to Jamie. She may also have altered the tone of her voice slightly for each speaker. The point is that the narrator can easily differentiate for the listener which speaker said what.

ASL is able to make the same distinctions, and one way is to move the body into different spaces to represent different signers. If we translated the earlier dialogue into ASL, it might look like this:

So Jamie says to me, "I have to use the car tomorrow."

S-O J-A-M-I-E TELL-ME TOMORROW PRO-1 MUST USE CAR

I respond, "You do? I thought you didn't need it."

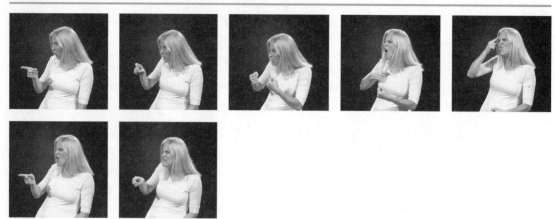

PRO-X NEED CAR PRO-1 THINK PRO-X NOT NEED

He replies, "I didn't think I did, but something has come up."

PRO-1 THINK NOT SOMETHING COME-UP NEED

Notice how the narrator shifts her body—in particular, how the angle of her shoulders alters—to distinguish when she is producing signs that represent Jamie's words and those that represent hers.

INDICATING DIFFERENT TOPICS

A second way ASL signers use body language is to distinguish between topics. As I will explain in subsequent chapters, the space around a signer can be associated with different concepts. If a person is comparing the pros and cons of two different sports, for example, a space to the right of the signer might be associated with one sport and the space to the left might be another sport. The signer can move her body into a different space as a signal that she is going to discuss a particular sport.

Here is an example of what this might look like:

I can't decide between two sports.

PRO-1 CAN'T DECIDE 2 SPORTS

There is snowboarding, and there is swimming.

PRO→|SNOWBOARD| (left) PRO→|SWIM| (right)

They each have pros and cons.

EACH HAVE POSITIVE NEGATIVE

For example, snowboarding . . .

EXAMPLE shift (left) SNOWBOARD . . .

The signer first establishes the two areas in space and what they will be associated with, for example, PRO→SNOWBOARD (left) PRO→SWIM (right). Then when she wants to talk about the topic of snowboarding, she moves her body into the appropriate space to signal that her comments are going to be associated with that sport.

In more formal discourse situations, such as a lecture, signers often move their entire body between two areas. Suppose the signer is a snowboarding coach and is recruiting students at a high school to join her squad. The sequence might look something like this:

Perhaps you can't decide between two sports.

MAYBE PRO-X CAN'T-DECIDE 2 SPORTS

There is snowboarding, and there is swimming.

SNOWBOARD (left extended point) PRO→SWIM (right extended point)

Each has pros and cons.

EACH HAVE POSITIVE NEGATIVE

For example, snowboarding . . .

EXAMPLE (walk to the left) SNOWBOARD . . .

In this example the presenter again associates the space to her left with snowboarding and the space to her right with swimming. Notice that when she points this time, her arm is extended farther than it was in the first example:

There is snowboarding, and there is swimming.

PRO→SNOWBOARD (left) compared with PRO→SWIM (right extended point) COMPARE

This is because she is using not only the area immediately in front of her on the left, but the entire space to her left, as the area associated with snowboarding. Then when she wants to talk about this sport, she actually walks to that area and begins signing. Later she can walk to the right side and talk about swimming.

DEMONSTRATING AN ACTION

ASL can capitalize on the fact that it is a visual language by using body language to demonstrate actions. The body is used to mimic movements that it might actually perform. I use the words *mimic* and *demonstrate* because signers don't normally replicate the movements exactly. For example, if someone is describing a 5K race in which she recently competed, she might produce the following sequence:

Last week I competed in a 5K race.

LAST-WEEK PRO-1 COMPETE 5-K

I started to run.

PRO-1 START RUN

In the final sequence of photos, the narrator moves her arms forward and backward in a way similar to that of a runner. However, the arm swing is greatly abbreviated, and the arms themselves are higher than if she had actually been running.

Another difference between the demonstration of how she ran and what it actually looked like is that she never moves her legs. The narrator is able to use her body to partially demonstrate what she looked like while running to give the viewer a feel for the process, but she did not get up and actually start running around the room. Using the body to demonstrate actions is a common way of conveying movement in ASL.

DEMONSTRATING A CHARACTER

A final way that the body may be used is to demonstrate how a character might look or act. This is an extension of how the face can be used to demonstrate a character, and the two are often used simultaneously. Let's continue with our previous narrative about the runner who competed in a 5K race. Suppose that, despite her best efforts, she did not win. It would be possible for her to demonstrate her reaction not only with her face, but with her entire body. For example:

I tried my best, but I lost.

TRY HARD LOST

I was disappointed.

PRO-1 DISAPPOINT (hunch shoulders)

You can see how the signer uses her entire body to express her disappointment—her shoulders are hunched and her head hangs down.

Chapter Summary

Signers depend on their faces and bodies to contribute meaning to most of their utterances. It is important to pay attention to how this occurs and begin to practice using your facial expressions and body language as you learn sign vocabulary. If you focus on just memorizing lexical signs, you will not learn to produce grammatical ASL properly. Your face and body must be incorporated if you are to be successful.

In this chapter, you learned the following:

1. How facial expressions are used to identify basic sentence structures.
2. How facial expressions are used to express grammatical aspect.
3. How facial expressions are used to express emotive information.
4. How facial expressions are used to provide discursive information.
5. How facial expressions are used to convey a character.
6. How the body is used to produce lexical signs.
7. How the body is used to indicate different signers.
8. How the body is used to indicate different topics in a discussion.
9. How the body is used to demonstrate a physical action.
10. How the body is used to demonstrate a character.

QUIZ

1. True or false: Facial expressions are used to identify basic sentence structures in ASL.
2. True or false: ASL does not use facial expression for emotive information.
3. True or false: ASL uses facial expressions to convey discursive information.
4. True or false: ASL uses facial expressions to convey how a character in a story might look.
5. True or false: The body is used to produce signs in ASL.
6. True or false: The body cannot be used to indicate two different signers in ASL.
7. True or false: ASL signers can move their bodies to indicate different topics.

8. True or false: The body cannot be used to demonstrate an action or physical movement in ASL.

9. True or false: The body can be used to demonstrate how a character might look or act in ASL.

10. True or false: The use of the face and body are not necessary to produce grammatical ASL.

CHAPTER 3

Grammar and Sentence Structure

When people think of the term *grammar*, they most often think of the rules for producing grammatically correct sentences. Grammar actually has a broader definition when used by linguists: it is the study of the rules governing the use of a language. Languages have rules to create individuals parts (for spoken languages, these are the sounds), to create words, and to create sentences. Studies in these different areas are referred to as phonology, morphology, and syntax, respectively. This chapter looks at the phonology, morphology, and syntax of ASL.

ASL Phonology

Phonology is the study of the smallest contrastive units of language. For spoken languages, those units are sounds. In ASL, they include hand configurations, movements, locations, and orientations.

STOKOE'S WORK

Chapter 1 outlined William Stokoe's work as it related to the phonology of signs. He demonstrated how each individual sign is created from a combination of three things—a handshape, a location, and a movement—and that this combination of parts parallels how words in spoken languages can be broken down into component parts. Each of the component parts has a finite number of ways in which it can be produced. Stokoe identified an inventory of parts and assigned a symbol to represent each one (Table 3.1).

Table 3.1   Stokoe Notations and Description of Sign Parts (From *A Dictionary of American Sign Language* by Stokoe, Casterline, and Croneberg, Sign Media.)

	Symbol	Description
Handshape	B	Flat hand
	A	Compact hand, fist; may be like *a*, *s*, or *t* of manual alphabet
	G/1	Index, hand; like *g*, or sometimes *d* of manual alphabet; index finger points from fist
	C	Curved hand; may be like *c* of manual alphabet or more open
	5	Spread hand; fingers and thumb spread like *5* of manual numeration
	V	Index and second fingers extended and spread apart
	O	Tapered hand; fingers curved and squeezed together over thumb; may be like *o* of manual alphabet
	F	From spread hand, thumb and index finger touch or cross
	X	Hook hand; index finger bent in hook from fist, thumb tip may touch fingertip
	H	Index and second fingers side-by-side, extended
	L	Angle hand; thumb and index finger in right angle, other fingers usually bent into palm
	Y	"Horns" hand; thumb and little finger spread out and extended from fist; or index and little fingers extended and parallel
	∝	Second finger bent in from spread hand, thumb may touch fingertip
	K	Like G except that thumb touches the second finger; like *k* and *p* of manual alphabet
	I	"Pinkie" hand; little finger extended from compact hand
	R	Second finger crossed over index finger; like *r* of manual alphabet
	W	Three-finger hand; thumb and little finger touch, others extended and spread
	3	Thumb and first two fingers spread, like *3* of manual numeration
	E	Contracted hand; like *e* of manual alphabet or more clawlike

continued

Table 3.1 Stokoe Notations and Description of Sign Parts *continued*

	Symbol	Description
Location	∅	Zero, the neutral place where the hands move, in contrast with all places below
	O	Face or whole head
	∩	Forehead or brow, upper face
	Δ	Midface, the eye and nose region
	∪	Chin, lower face
	}	Cheek, temple, ear, side of face
	Π	Neck
	[ ]	Trunk, body from shoulders to hips
	\	Upper arm
	√	Elbow, forearm
	σ	Wrist, arm in supinated position (palm up)
	σ	Wrist, arm in pronated position (palm down)
Movement	∧	Upward movement
	∨	Downward movement
	N	Up-and-down movement
	<	Rightward movement
	>	Leftward movement
	z	Side-to-side movement
	T	Movement toward signer
	⊥	Movement away from signer
	I	Back-and-forth movement
	a	Supinating rotation (palm up)
	□	Pronating rotation (palm down)
	ω	Twisting movement
	η	Nodding or bending action
	@	Circular action
	□	Opening action (final handshape shown in brackets)
	#	Closing action (final handshape shown in brackets)
	e	Wiggling action of fingers
	)(	Convergent action, approach
	×	Contractual action, touch
	Ⅱ	Linking action, grasp
	t	Crossing action
	⊙	Entering action
	÷	Divergent action, separate
	""	Interchanging action
	●	Repeated

Stokoe asserted that all signs could be broken into these three components. Let's examine a sign such as THANK-YOU to get a better understanding of his system.

THANK-YOU

First, we need to identify the location where the sign is produced. The sign THANK-YOU could be described as having two locations, the first at the chin and the second in neutral space. Stokoe focused on the initial location only and therefore would have described the location as "chin, lower face" and represented this location with the symbol ∪.

Second, let's identify the handshape used in the articulation of the sign. Stokoe would describe this handshape as a "flat hand" and would represent it with the symbol B.

Finally, we want to describe the movement used as the sign is articulated. It begins at the chin and moves away from the signer. The symbol to represent this movement is ⊥.

Following Stokoe's practice of writing the location first, followed by the handshape and then the movement, the sign THANK-YOU would be represented in Stokoe notation as ∪ B ⊥.

Stokoe's contribution of demonstrating how signs had three component parts was invaluable to the understanding of sign languages. However, his conception of how signs were produced was that the parts were produced simultaneously rather than in a specified sequence. If this were true, it would make the fundamental structure of sign language different from that of spoken languages, whose parts are produced sequentially. More on this point in a moment.

LIDDELL AND JOHNSON

In the early 1980s, as Stokoe's tenure at Gallaudet University was winding down (he retired in 1984), two linguists arrived. The first, Robert E. Johnson, was retained by the university to establish a linguistics department, and in this capacity, he began to hire faculty members for the fledgling department. One such faculty member was Scott K. Liddell. The two had been working independently for several years on the phonological systems of ASL with some success. However, it was when they were able to work together that they introduced a more complete understanding of the phonological structure of signs.

Liddell and Johnson's contribution was to demonstrate that signs, like words, are created from parts that are arranged sequentially. Let's begin with the spoken English word *pat*. It is composed of three segments of sound / p /, / æ /, and / t /. It is possible to describe how each of these sounds are made. When describing consonants, we must identify the place of articulation, the manner of articulation, and whether or not the voice is used during articulation. Vowels are articulated, and therefore described, differently. Vowels are described by identifying the tongue height, tongue advancement, lip rounding, and whether the tongue and lips are tense or lax. The order of the three sounds is important as well. If we rearrange the sounds into / t /, / æ /, / p /, a new word (*tap*) is created, which has a different meaning than *pat*.

Each segment of sound is made of a specific group of features. If any one of the features in the segment is changed, the sound is produced differently. Let's compare the spoken English words *pat* and *bat*. Table 3.2 identifies the features for producing each sound.

Table 3.2   Comparison of the Pronunciation of *Pat* and *Bat*

Pat

	/ p /	/ æ /	/ t /
Place of articulation	Bilabial	Low, lax, front	Alveolar
Manner of articulation	Stop	Stop	
Voiced/voiceless	**Voiceless**		Voiceless

Bat

	/ b /	/ æ /	/ t /
Place of articulation	Bilabial	Low, lax, front	Alveolar
Manner of articulation	Stop		Stop
Voiced/voiceless:	**Voiced**		Voiceless

The / p / segment, for instance, has three features: bilabial, stop, and voiceless. When we alter one feature, we can change how the sound is articulated. So the / p / sound changes to / b / when the voice is used to produce it. In English, this difference results in the meaning of the word changing from "to tap or stroke gently with the hand" to "a sharp blow." The individual features in each segment create the particular sound, and the order or sequence of the segments create words.

Liddell and Johnson showed that signs also are sequentially produced. In other words, the order in which parts are articulated is significant. If we look at the sign THANK-YOU again, we can better understand their point. When making the sign THANK-YOU, we begin with the hand near the mouth and end with the hand away from the mouth.

Suppose we changed this sequence and began with the hand away from the mouth and ended at the mouth. It would look something like this:

*THANK-YOU

This no longer has the meaning "to be grateful." In fact there are no signs in ASL that are made this way. It is an ungrammatical, nonexistent sign.

Liddell and Johnson proposed that a more accurate analysis of signs is one in which they are described as a series of postures and transitions. *Postures* are segments in which the features are static. *Transitions* are segments in which the features change. The linguists also described how each segment is produced. It requires a hand configuration, placement of the hand, and the direction the hand is facing. Table 3.3 illustrates what this would look like.

Table 3.3   THANK-YOU

	P	**T**	**P**
Hand configuration	b1234		b1234
Placement of hand	At chin	Changing	Anterior chin
Direction of hand	Supine		Supine

The sign can be broken into three segments (P, T, and P), and the features that are part of each segment can be described. The parallels with spoken English are apparent. While English combines consonants and vowels to create words, ASL uses postures and transitions to create signs.

ASL signs, like words, comprise a series of segments that are produced sequentially. The segments are a cluster of features—hand configuration, placement of the hand, and direction of the hand—that can be described.

ASL Morphology

Now that you have an understanding of how ASL builds individual signs, we can look at how it creates more complex words. Morphology is the study of how languages combine morphemes to form complex words. *Morphemes* are meaningful parts of words and signs that cannot be further subdivided without a loss of meaning. In English, a word such as *houses* is made from two morphemes. The first, *house*, means a building that serves as living quarters. The second, *-s*, means more than one. We can't further subdivide the word *house*. For instance, English doesn't have a meaning attached to the unit *hou*. Some morphemes are *free*, meaning they are grammatical units that can occur by themselves, such as *house*. Other morphemes, like *-s*, are *bound*, meaning they are grammatical units that can never occur by themselves; they must be attached to some other morpheme.

    ASL is able to build signs from smaller morphemes as well. In the following sections I will introduce you to several of these more complex forms.

PREFIXES AND SUFFIXES

You are probably familiar with prefixes and suffixes. Prefixes are bound morphemes that are joined to the beginning of a root morpheme. *Un-* is an example of a prefix in English and has the meaning "not, opposite of." When this bound morpheme is joined to a free morpheme like *happy*, you create a new complex word—*unhappy*.

    Suffixes are bound morphemes that are joined to the end of a root morpheme. An example of an English suffix is *-ness*, which means "a state or quality." If you take the root morpheme *happy* again and add the suffix *-ness*, you get the new complex word *happiness*.

    ASL uses prefixes and suffixes to create more complex signs; however, their use is more limited than in English. ASL has a prefix that means "age of living thing." It attaches to numeral signs and is used to express age. The prefix is made through initial contact with the chin and is followed by a numeral sign. The following example demonstrates a signer making the sign that means "three years old."

{AGE$_0$}—THREE

The initial contact of the pointer finger of the handshape for THREE to the chin is the prefix, which is glossed as {AGE$_0$}. The numeral sign THREE is the root morpheme. In Chapter 13, I will explain in more detail how this prefix is used in conjunction with other numbers. You can skip to that chapter now if you want to learn different ways of expressing age.

The suffix in ASL that is glossed -ER adds the meaning of "agent nominalizer" to verbs. It is produced by making two B handshapes with the palms facing one another about shoulder-width apart and moving down from about the signer's shoulders to the trunk. The formation of the -ER suffix is illustrated here:

-ER

Although the gloss -ER is similar to the English suffix *-er*, the ASL suffix -ER has fewer root morphemes to which it can attach. Unlike the English suffix *-er*, which is highly productive (meaning it can attach to many English verbs to form nouns), -ER is much more restricted. For instance, in English we can add *-er* to the verb *tickle* and create the word *tickler* to refer to the person performing the action of tickling. ASL would not use the -ER suffix in the same way. The following photos show a few complex signs that are produced by adding the -ER suffix to a verb:

TEACHER

DRIVER

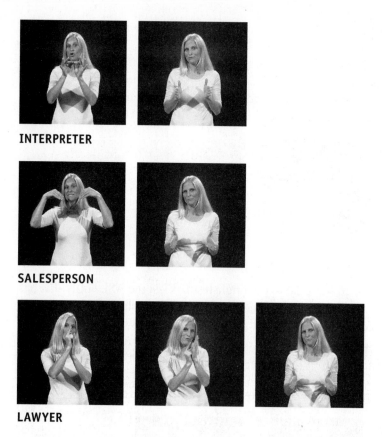

INTERPRETER

SALESPERSON

LAWYER

(For the signs for MANAGER, ACCOUNTANT, SERVER/WAITER, WRITER, SUPERVISOR, or WORKER, see the DVD.)

These are the only prefixes and suffixes in ASL, so it is apparent that using prefixes and suffixes is not how ASL produces complex signs. A much more common way is internal modification to the form of a sign and the use of reduplication, which will be explained later. Recall that Chapter 1 mentioned how important it is to learn the structures in a language that produce equivalent meaning. This is one example of where that is true. While English speakers are used to using prefixes and suffixes to create more complex words, this structure is not prevalent in ASL. Of course, if you compared the English prefix and suffix system to that of another language such as German, the English system would seem limited. Each language draws on different structures to different degrees. As you progress through this book, you will learn other structures used by ASL signers (many of which are not used in English) to produce complex signs.

ASL PRONOUNS

Pronouns are words or signs that replace a noun. In English, for example, I might say, "Jamie plays hockey. He has a game this weekend." The word *he* in the second sentence replaces the noun *Jamie* in the first. A personal pronoun in English refers to a specific thing and changes (through inflection) its form to indicate a person, number, gender, and case. The decision as to what a pronoun can indicate varies by language. French, for instance, has inflections to indicate the following: role in the sentence (subject, direct object, and so on), person, gender, number, and familiarity. The result is that French has more pronouns than English.

Pronouns in ASL can indicate person and number. ASL only identifies first person and non–first person. While English has a separate form for first person (*I/me* for singular, *we* for plural), second person (*you*), and third person (*he/she/it* singular, *they* plural), ASL collapses these into just two categories:

First Person *Singular*	Non–First Person
I	**You**

PRO-1   PRO→X

My	**Yours**

POSS-1   POSS

Myself

SELF-ONLY-1

Yourself

SELF-ONLY

Myself (emphatic)

SELF-ONLY-1!

Yourself (emphatic)

SELF-ONLY!

Person being described is . . .

SELF-CHAR

I
(formal, no English equivalent)

You
(formal, no English equivalent)

PRO-FORMAL-1

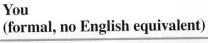

PRO-FORMAL

Dual

The two of us

The two of them

PRO-DUAL-1

PRO-DUAL

Multiple (Pronouns Referring to Three or More People)

The three of us

The three of them

{PRO-MULTI-1}{THREE}

{PRO-MULTI}{THREE}

The four of us

{PRO-MULTI-1}{FOUR}

The four of them

{PRO-MULTI}{FOUR}

The five of us

{PRO-MULTI-1}{FIVE}

The five of them

{PRO-MULTI}{FIVE}

The six of us

{PRO-MULTI-1}{SIX}

The six of them

{PRO-MULTI}{SIX}

The seven of us

{PRO-MULTI-1}{SEVEN}

The seven of them

{PRO-MULTI}{SEVEN}

The eight of us

{PRO-MULTI-1}{EIGHT}

The eight of them

{PRO-MULTI}{EIGHT}

The nine of us

{PRO-MULTI-1}{NINE}

The nine of them

{PRO-MULTI}{NINE}

Plural

We

PRO-PL-1 (WE)

You
(plural, no English equivalent)

PRO-PL (YOU)

Our

POSS-PL-1 (OUR)

Your/their

POSS-PL

Exclusive group,
including the signer

SELF-ONLY-PL-1

Exclusive group,
not including the signer

SELF-ONLY-PL

Them (formal, no English equivalent)

PRO-FORMAL-PL

ASPECT

A final way ASL can create more complex signs is by changing the form of the sign. These changes can be accomplished through reduplication, which are internal changes in the form of the sign.

Reduplication is used to add meaning to a word or sign through a specific type of repetition. English does not use reduplication to create complex words, but many other spoken languages do. Malay, for example, uses reduplication of a noun to indicate the plural. For example, *buku* means "book"; when it is reduplicated as *buku-buku*, it means "books."

ASL employs the use of reduplication in two ways. The first is used with signs referring to time. The reduplication adds the meaning of "every *x*" where *x* is the unit of time being discussed. To express the meaning "three months," you produce the sign:

{MONTH}{THREE}

Now, if you wanted to express the idea that something is to happen every three months, the sign would be repeated as follows:

{MONTH}{THREE}[EVERY]

Another example would be changing the sign that expresses the meaning "one week" and adding reduplication so that it means "every week":

{WEEK}{ONE}

{WEEK}{ONE}[EVERY]

Verbs can also be reduplicated to express aspectual information (duration, frequency, manner, or repetitiveness). Let's use the sign LOOK-AT to see how reduplication is used to change the meaning of a verb. The basic form of the sign LOOK-AT looks like this:

LOOK-AT

If you wanted to add the meaning "incessantly (over a short period of time)," you would change the form of the verb by repeating the movement:

LOOK-AT

The verb can be changed in a third way to create a more complex sign that means "to look at something again and again with regularity." It would look like this:

LOOK-AT

Notice that there is a slight circular motion added that the "incessant" form did not have.

If the action occurred over an extended period of time, this fourth form of the verb would look like this:

LOOK-AT

When the verb is reduplicated in this case, the circular motion is larger than for the form meaning "repeated regularly."

Finally, you could reduplicate the sign in the following way:

LOOK-AT

The form changes again in that there is a combination of the straight path away from the signer, plus a circling back. This form gives the meaning of something happening over time but with the feeling of it being unnecessary or unexpected.

Notice that in the production of these more complex forms of the signs that the reduplication is also accompanied by a change in facial expression. It is important to remember that several linguistic components often occur simultaneously in the articulation of a single sign.

Throughout this book, you will see additional examples of reduplication. This is one of the more highly productive ways in which ASL creates more complex signs. It can be one of the more challenging parts of the language for people who speak English because English does not have a similar structure.

ASL Syntax

You will learn many different lexical signs as you progress through this book. Once you have an available vocabulary, you will want to link these signs together to create sentences. In this section, I will outline the basic rules of ASL syntax that will allow you to accomplish this.

ASL relies on both facial expression and the order of signs to produce grammatically correct sentences. If you attempt to analyze an ASL sentence without accounting for the contribution of facial expression, or nonmanual signal (NMS), you will arrive at an incorrect sentence structure. I will first outline the types of nonmanual signals used in ASL sentences. Then I will explain the possible word orders that are available.

USING NONMANUAL SIGNALS TO PRODUCE DIFFERENT TYPES OF SENTENCES

Nonmanual signals are used to indicate different sentences in ASL. If you were making a declarative statement, such as "You are home," you could express that in ASL with the following sentence:

PRO HOME

The signer has what we call a neutral facial expression; it is unmarked in any way. You may also note that ASL does not sign "are." ASL does not have a verb that is equivalent to the English "to be."

To ask a question that can be answered by either yes or no, the word order stays the same, but the nonmanual sign changes. The signer's eyebrows are raised, the head and upper torso lean slightly forward, and the eyes may be widened as the signs are produced:

y/n
―――――
PRO HOME

When glossing the sentence, the nonmanual sign is indicated by drawing a line above the signs with which the NMS is produced and then a symbol identifying the type of NMS used. In this example, the glossed sentence would look like this:

y/n
―――――――――
PRO HOME

Some questions require more than a yes/no answer. These types of questions are referred to as "WH- questions." In English, we use the words *who, what, when, where, why,* or *how* in these questions. ASL has lexical signs for these concepts as well (you will learn more about them and other types of questions in Chapter 8). In addition, however, the question must be produced with the correct nonmanual signal. In the nonmanual signal that accompanies WH- questions, the eyebrows are furrowed, and the head and torso are shifted slightly forward. If I wanted to ask the question, "Where do you live?" it could be signed as follows:

<u>   wh   </u>
LIVE WHERE PRO

Some sentences require negation. The English sentence "I do not understand," for instance, would be signed as follows:

<u>   neg </u>
PRO-1 UNDERSTAND

As the signer produces the signs

<u>   neg </u>
PRO-1 UNDERSTAND

she also shakes her head. This headshake negates the sentence. The sign NOT may or may not be used, unlike in English, which requires the word *not* to create a negative sentence; ASL can use the nonmanual signal alone. The use of a lexical sign is optional, but the headshake is required.

Another nonmanual signal is one that marks topics. An ASL topic is a separate clause in a sentence and is used to identify what the topic of the sentence is. To produce this nonmanual signal, you raise your eyebrows and tilt your head back slightly. Here is an example of this type of sentence:

t

POSS-1 PAPER PRO-1 FINISH

Notice that the nonmanual signal occurs only with the first two signs, and then a neutral expression is used. An English translation of this sentence is "As for my paper, I finished it." While this type of sentence structure is possible, it is not often used in spoken English. In ASL, however, topicalized (where the signer is identifying a topic that he will then comment about) sentences are used to introduce new topics into discourse.

A nonmanual signal that is similar to the one to mark topics is that to mark a conditional sentence, but the latter differs in that it is also accompanied by a head and torso tilt that is slightly upward and to the side. Conditional sentences are those that have an "if-then" situation. For example, "If it rains tomorrow, the game will be canceled." The equivalent of this sentence in ASL would look like this:

cond

TOMORROW RAIN GAME CANCEL

The NMS looks nearly like the one used to mark topics: the eyebrows are raised, the head is tilted, and the nonmanual signal only occurs with the first two signs, TOMORROW and RAIN—the "if" portion of the sentence.

A final nonmanual signal is used when giving a command, such as "Sit down!" This NMS is produced while maintaining direct eye contact with the addressee and a frown or serious expression. Asterisks before and after the gloss indicate the NMS for command is used.

SIT

Nonmanual signals are required in ASL if you are to produce grammatically correct sentences. Another component to this is using appropriate word order, which we will look at now.

ASL WORD ORDER

Most people are familiar with the concepts of subject, verb, and object. A subject (S) is the primary actor in a sentence. The verb (V) is an action or state of something. An object (O) is the receiver of an action. Every language has different rules about the order in which these three elements occur. The basic word order in English is subject-verb-object (SVO). ASL shares this same basic word order, but there are a number of significant variations from English.

Let's begin with an example of the basic SVO word order:

PRO-1 READ BOOK

This sentence can be translated into English as "I read the book." (It should be pointed out that the use of articles such as *a*, *an*, and *the* is different in ASL than in English, but be aware that the use of a determiner is far less frequent in ASL than in English.) The subject, PRO-1, is the signer; the verb, READ, is the action of reading; and the object, BOOK, is the receiver of the action.

Here are some additional examples:

GIRL PLAY VOLLEYBALL

MOTHER CLEAN HOUSE

BOY WATCH #TV

This basic word order is very common and gives you a basic structure to work with when creating sentences. However, a number of other possibilities can also be used.

The second possible word order is verb-object (VO). Most English speakers find this one unusual because English almost never has a sentence in which the subject is not overt (mentioned). The verb system in English contributes to this. In English, only third person singular verbs are marked. Look at the following:

I arrive	We arrive
You arrive	You (pl) arrive
He/she/it arrives	They arrive

The -s on the verb marks the third person singular form. The conjugations of verbs in other languages, however, have a different form for each person. Here are the conjugations for the Spanish verb *llegar* ("to arrive"):

First person singular	*llego*	First person plural	*llegamos*
Second person singular	*llegas*	Second person plural	*llegáis*
Third person singular	*llega*	Third person plural	*llegan*

In Spanish, the verb form changes depending on the subject. It is unnecessary to always identify the subject, because this information can be discerned from the verb form. This isn't possible in English; hence, English speakers must have an overt subject.

In ASL, you can have a sentence with just a verb and an object if the subject has already been mentioned in the discourse (for example, in the prior sentence). It is also possible to identify the subject based on the signer's body position. Here are a couple of examples:

PRO-1 BORROW BOOK. READ BOOK

BOY RECEIVE BALL PRO-X. KICK BALL

In the first example, PRO-1 BORROW BOOK. READ BOOK, the first sentence is in SVO word order. These sentences are translated as "I borrowed the book. I read the book." The second sentence is VO word order. The subject of the second sentence is not overtly marked with a sign but is understood from the first sentence to be PRO-1, or "I." The second example, BOY RECEIVE BALL. KICK BALL would be translated as "The boy received the ball. He then kicked the ball." The signer establishes the area to her right as "the boy." When she moves her body into that space, she essentially takes on the role of the boy and demonstrates what he does. She can simply sign KICK BALL because it is understood from the body shift that she is in the role of "boy."

A third sentence structure that is used in ASL is topic-verb-object (TVO). This structure uses the nonmanual signal for topic to identify what the sentence will be about, and then the remainder of the sentence comments on this topic. For instance,

POSS-1 DAUGHTER LOVE ICE-CREAM

WOMAN THERE WRITE BOOK

The English translation of the first example,

$$\overline{\text{POSS-1 DAUGHTER LOVE}}^{\,t}\text{ ICE-CREAM}$$

is "As for my daughter, she loves ice cream." The signer identified the topic as "my daughter" using the nonmanual signal of raised eyebrows and a slight head tilt, then she comments about her daughter with the verb LOVE and object ICE-CREAM. The second example,

$$\overline{\text{WOMAN THERE}}^{\,t}\text{ WRITE BOOK}$$

translates to "The woman over there, she is the one who wrote the book." Again, the topic is identified—in this situation, a particular woman. Then the signer comments about that person. However, the signer is not obligated to overtly produce a subject because the topic has already identified what will be discussed.

You might assume that topics simply function as subjects, but this isn't the case, as the following examples illustrate. The word order in these examples is topic-subject-verb (TSV):

$\overline{\text{BOOK THERE}}^{\text{t}}$ **PRO-1 READ**

$\overline{\text{BASKETBALL}}^{\text{t}}$ **PRO-1 PLAY**

In these examples, the topic is identified and then the signer explains something about her involvement with it. In the first example,

$$\overline{\text{BOOK THERE}}^{\text{t}} \text{ PRO-1 READ}$$

which translates to "That book there, I read it," the book is identified as the topic, then the signer states that she read it. In the second example,

$$\overline{\text{BASKETBALL}}^{\text{t}} \text{ PRO-1 PLAY}$$

means "As for basketball, I play it." Again the topic of basketball is identified, then the signer comments on her involvement with the sport.

A fifth word order that is used in ASL is called subject–verb–pronoun-copy (SVPro-Copy). What is different about this structure is the pronoun-copy, which means the signer produces a pronoun that refers back to the subject of the sentence. The production of this pronoun is most often accompanied by a head nod. Here is an example of the SVPro-Copy word order:

MAN QUIT PRO-COPY

The English translation of this sentence is "The man quit." The final sign, PRO, is used to emphasize that the signer is talking about the man.

A related word order is verb–pro-copy (VPro-Copy). Like the VO word order discussed earlier, the subject in this type of sentence is not overtly produced. What or whom is being discussed is understood from the previous discourse. Here is an example of the VPro-Copy word order:

GIRL CRY WHY. FALL PRO-COPY

This example has two sentences. In the first,

$$\overset{\text{rh}}{\text{GIRL CRY }\overline{\text{WHY}}}$$

means "Why is the girl crying?" The signer produces FALL PRO in the second sentence, which would be translated as "The girl fell." The second sentence does not produce an overt subject, rather the subject is understood to be "the girl" from the prior sentence. The pro-copy refers back to this subject.

The final common word order is one that was used in the last example,

$$\overset{\text{rh}}{\text{GIRL CRY }\overline{\text{WHY}};}$$

it is subject-verb (SV). It is possible to have a sentence without an object, whether because the verb is intransitive (meaning it does not accept a direct object) or simply because the decision is made not to identify the object.

As you can see, ASL has a number of word order options. Some are similar to those found in English (SVO, SV), while others are not (VO, TSV, TVO, SVPro-

Copy, VPro-Copy). From these basic structures, you can create more complex sentences (more about that in upcoming chapters). What is important to remember is that for several of the sentence structures, nonmanual signals are necessary to identify the correct word order.

Chapter Summary

In this chapter, you learned the rules for producing grammatically correct ASL and were introduced to the rules governing the phonology, morphology, and syntax. These included the following:

1. Individual signs are produced sequentially. Signs are made from a series of postures and transitions.

2. The individual features of postures and transitions can be described in detail. A change to a single feature may result in the production of a new sign.

3. Morphemes are the smallest meaningful units in a language. Free morphemes can occur by themselves. Bound morphemes must attach to a root morpheme.

4. Prefixes and suffixes in ASL are limited. One prefix is the $\{AGE_0\}$, which means "age of living." A suffix that is used to nominalize some verbs is the -ER morpheme, which is similar to the -er morpheme in English but has a much more limited use.

5. ASL has first person and non–first person pronouns.

6. ASL pronouns mark person and number.

7. Reduplication is a highly productive way in which ASL creates more complex signs.

8. Nonmanual signals (NMS) are required to produce grammatical sentences and distinguish different sentence types. These sentence types and associated nonmanual signals are as follows:

    • Declarative sentence—neutral facial expression
    • Yes-or-no questions—raised eyebrows
    • WH- questions—lowered eyebrows
    • Topicalized sentence—raised eyebrows, head tilt
    • Conditional sentence—raised eyebrows, head tilt
    • Command—furrowed eyebrows, direct eye contact

9. Word order in ASL is fixed, although there are a number of possible options:

- SVO
- VO
- TSV
- TVO
- SVPro-Copy
- VPro-Copy

QUIZ

1. True or false: Grammar is the study of rules governing the use of a language.

2. What are the Stokoe Notation symbols for the following handshapes?

    (a) Flat hand
    (b) Index and second fingers extended and spread apart
    (c) Index and second fingers extended and side-by-side

3. What are the Stokoe Notation symbols for the following locations?

    (a) Face or whole head
    (b) Chin or lower face
    (c) Forehead, eyebrow, or upper face

4. What are the Stokoe Notation symbols for the following movements?

    (a) Upward movement
    (b) Movement away from the signer
    (c) Repeated movement

5. True or false: Signs are produced sequentially.

6. True or false: Morphology is the study of how languages combine morphemes to form complex words.

7. True or false: ASL has different pronouns that identify first, second, and third person.

8. True or false: ASL uses reduplication to add meaning to a sign through a specific type of repetition.

9. True or false: The basic word order in ASL is object-subject-verb (OSV).

10. True or false: Verb-object (VO) is one possible word order in ASL.

CHAPTER 4

Verbs

Regardless of the language you choose to learn, the most complex part is the verb system. It is far easier to learn words or signs for nouns, because these tend to be static items that change in limited ways (becoming plural, for example). Verbs, however, can be inflected for tense, aspect, and voice, and they have to agree with other aspects of a sentence such as person, number, or grammatical gender. They assert something about the subject of the sentence and express actions, events, or states of being.

ASL verbs convey the same types of information as verbs in other languages. The significant difference is the form they take and how they are changed to express different types of information. In this chapter, we will look at the three types of verbs that exist in ASL and how they are used. How a verb is produced is important in determining to which group it belongs.

All of the following examples can be found on the DVD, along with additional vocabulary and example sentences.

Plain Verbs

Plain verbs are produced in a static location, and the articulation of the sign cannot be altered. Altering the production of the verb will result in a different or an ungrammatical sign. Recall from Chapter 3 that signs are made up of different parts: handshape, location, movement, and orientation. In the articulation of verbs that are not plain verbs, these parts can be altered in various ways. Plain verbs, however, cannot be altered in any way; they are simply how the sign is produced. Additionally, plain verbs do not provide information about the subject or object. This means they are not marked or altered when they are produced to indicate such things as whether the subject of the sentence is singular or plural, or male or female.

Here is a list of plain verbs. Throughout this chapter, I will identify a verb with a gloss and provide its English translation since the meaning is not always clear from the gloss alone.

Eat—to consume food

EAT

Enjoy—to appreciate something, to experience pleasure or satisfaction

ENJOY

Forget—to be unable to recall

FORGET

Have—to possess

HAVE

Like—to be suitable or agreeable

LIKE

Love—to adore, to feel a strong attraction for another

LOVE

Know—to be aware of the truth or factuality of; to have a practical understanding of

KNOW

Think—to have a view or opinion

THINK

Dream—to have a dream, to consider a possibility

DREAM

Laugh—to show emotion

LAUGH

Plain verbs are different from the two other categories (indicating and depicting verbs) in that they cannot be directed in space or altered in any way without the sign becoming ungrammatical. This difference will become more apparent after you have read about the other two types of verbs. To illustrate this difference, let's attempt to alter the articulation of one of the plain verbs, ENJOY. In its grammatical form, the sign is made on the signer's torso. Suppose we changed the orientation of the hands so they were directed away from the body like this:

ENJOY

The sign is now ungrammatical for the sign meaning "to appreciate something, to experience pleasure or satisfaction." In fact, depending on the sentence in which it appears, it could mean "to wash or scrub something" or the lexical sign SUNDAY.

When using plain verbs, it is necessary to identify or to have already established through previous discourse who is performing or experiencing the action, since this information is not conveyed by the form of the verb. If a signer is identifying who has possession of something, for example, he would need to overtly identify the possessor. Suppose you wanted to express these two sentences: "I have the book," and "The girl has the book." You would articulate the verb HAVE the same way in both sentences. In addition, you would need to identify the subject.

I have the book.

PRO-1 HAVE BOOK

The girl has the book.

GIRL HAVE BOOK

It would be ungrammatical to change the direction of the sign HAVE to be directed in space toward an area associated with "the girl." For example:

GIRL *HAVE BOOK

You may have noticed that plain verbs often make contact with or are articulated near the body. This is one possible reason that altering their production is not allowed.

Indicating Verbs

Indicating verbs are more complex than plain verbs. They can be directed in space (moved toward or away from things) to incorporate additional information about the subject and/or object of the sentence.

Before continuing with the explanation of indicating verbs, I need to introduce another term, *citation form*. This refers to a sign articulated by a signer when she is asked what the sign is for a specific English verb. For example, if asked what the sign is for "give," the signer's response would look like this:

GIVE

The signer moves her hand from a position near the center of her torso to a position ahead of this point. GIVE is an indicating verb, but when it is not used in a sentence, a signer cannot direct it meaningfully because no information about the subject is known. Consequently, the citation form is produced. We can think of the citation form as the most basic form of a sign, the form that typically appears in an ASL dictionary. In everyday discourse, however, the citation form is rarely used. Let's return to the discussion of indicating verbs and see what actually happens.

Back in Chapter 1, I explained that what makes ASL so different from English is that the space around the signer can be associated with different meanings or entities. Signers frequently establish areas in the signing space around them with different meanings or entities. A simple example of this would look like the following:

GIRL THERE BOY THERE

The signer has established the area to her right with "the girl" by pointing in that direction and the area to her left with "the boy" by pointing to her left. Areas that have been associated with meaning are referred to as *tokens*.

Once a token has been established, the signer can direct signs toward or away from the area to indicate the entities' involvement. Returning to the verb GIVE, the signer could indicate that she gave something to "the girl" by signing GIVE$^{\rightarrow|girl|}$, which would look like this:

GIVE$^{\rightarrow|girl|}$

Because the sign GIVE began near the signer and ended near the area associated with "the girl," the meaning of the sentence is "I gave the girl." If, however, the signer changes how the sign is produced so it begins near the area associated with "the girl" and moves toward the signer, ending near her, the meaning of the sentence becomes "The girl gave me."

GIVE→|PRO-1|

The change in the starting and ending location of the sign provides additional information to the sentence. In fact, the verb incorporates enough information to allow a signer not to overtly produce a subject. Notice that in neither of the preceding examples, GIVE→|girl| or GIVE→|PRO-1|, does the signer produce a sign for the subject. This does not mean that an overt subject is ungrammatical; she could sign GIRL GIVE→|PRO-1|, and this would be an acceptable sentence. It just means that when using indicating verbs, it is possible to eliminate the overt production of the subject.

In these examples, one entity or person (the signer) was present, and one ("the girl") was not. It is also possible to indicate action when neither entity or person is actually present. Suppose the signer signed GIVE|girl|→|boy|, which would look like this:

GIVE|girl|→|boy|

This sentence means "The girl gave to the boy." Again, the verb is directed toward the two token spaces that have been established for "the girl" and "the boy." We understand that "the girl" is doing the giving and "the boy" is at the receiving end because the signer's hand begins near the area associated with "the girl" and moves left toward the area associated with "the boy."

You may have noticed that the gloss for GIVE→|girl| has some additional parts that weren't introduced in Chapter 1. Let me take a moment to explain this. There are conventions for writing signs that include information about how the sign is directed or placed in the signing space. These conventions are as follows:

1. PRO$^{\rightarrow x}$ This indicates that the sign is directed toward entity x. Entity x will either be something (such as another person) in the signer's environment or an entity (like the "boy" and "girl" from our GIVE example) associated with that space.

2. |girl| The word enclosed in vertical lines indicates the entity being identified.

3. GIVE$^{\rightarrow |girl|}$ The $^{\rightarrow |girl|}$ indicates that the sign is directed toward the area associated with |girl|.

4. GIVE$^{x \rightarrow y}$ The $^{x \rightarrow y}$ indicates that the sign begins nearer to and/or directed toward x and then moves toward y, where entity y is either something (such as another person) in the signer's environment or an entity associated with that space.

5. GIVE$^{x \leftarrow y}$ The $^{x \leftarrow y}$ indicates that the sign begins nearer to and/or directed toward y, then moves toward x.

6. INVITE$^{\leftarrow y}$ The $^{\leftarrow y}$ indicates that the verb begins directed toward y and then moves away from y.

7. GO$^{\rightarrow}$ The sign points in the direction of the action.

8. INFORM$^{[RECIP]x \leftrightarrow y}$ This indicates that the hands move in opposite directions between x and y. In this sign, each hand produces only a single movement. In producing a one-handed sign, such as SAME-DUAL$^{x \leftrightarrow y}$, the hand moves back and forth between x and y.

9. PRO-PL$^{\supset a,b,c}$ The $^{\supset a,b,c}$ indicates that the hand moves along a path such that the extent of the path points toward entities a, b, and c.

10. SAY-NO-TO$^{\cup x}$ The $^{\cup x}$ indicates that the head and eyes are directed toward entity x.

11. HONOR$^{\cup \rightarrow y}$ The $^{\cup \rightarrow y}$ indicates that the face and eyes ($\cup$), as well as the hands ($\rightarrow$), are directed toward y.

12. MOVE$^{L1 \rightarrow L2}$ The $^{L1 \rightarrow L2}$ indicates that the hand begins directed toward location 1 and ends directed toward location 2.

13. THROW$^{\rightarrow L}$ The sign is directed toward location L.

Here is a list of indicating verbs:

ADVISE⁻ʸ

ANSWER⁻ʸ

ASK-QUESTION⁻ʸ

BEG⁻ʸ

BITE⁻ʸ

BUY⁻ʸ

CALL-BY-PHONE⁻ʸ

FEED⁻ʸ

FORCE⁻ʸ

GIVE⁻ʸ

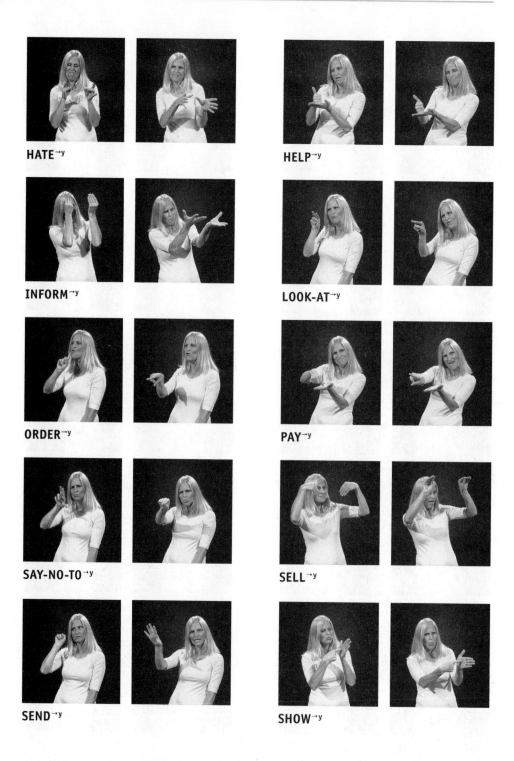

HATE⁻ʸ

HELP⁻ʸ

INFORM⁻ʸ

LOOK-AT⁻ʸ

ORDER⁻ʸ

PAY⁻ʸ

SAY-NO-TO⁻ʸ

SELL⁻ʸ

SEND⁻ʸ

SHOW⁻ʸ

SPELL-TO⁻ʸ

TELL⁻ʸ

WARN⁻ʸ

Indicating verbs can also be used to indicate the involvement of more than two entities in a situation. Suppose a teacher has a group of students sitting around her in a semicircle while they discuss some class material. She will likely ask them questions. If she wants to ask a question of the students on her left, she can direct the indicating verb ASK-QUESTION so it moves toward those students. For example,

ASK-QUESTION [MULTIPLE] ᵓᵃ,ᵇ,ᶜ

The signer moves her hand in a slight arc toward the students she is quizzing when she signs ASK-QUESTION [MULTIPLE] ᵓᵃ,ᵇ,ᶜ. The direction of the verb indicates who the object of the sentence is—in this case, the students on her left.

You are probably beginning to see how complex the ASL verb system is. Reciprocal verbs are another type of indicating verb. What makes them different from the ones we have discussed up to this point is that you use both hands at the same time to articulate the verb.

Remember the "boy" and "girl" the signer established in space in our earlier example? Let's return to them to illustrate the use of reciprocal verbs. In this new scenario, the boy and girl want to give each other something. In ASL, this would be expressed with the reciprocal verb GIVE[RECIP]|boy|↔|girl|.

GIVE[RECIP]|boy|↔|girl|

The signer's left hand starts on her left near the area associated with "the boy." Her right hand starts on her right near the area associated with "the girl." She then moves her hands so they cross paths in the middle and finish on the opposite side. It is as if you can visually see the girl handing an object to the boy and vice versa. A number of verbs can be used as reciprocal verbs, including the following:

GIVE[RECIP]x↔|y

SIGN-SPELL-TO[RECIP]x↔|y

HATE[RECIP]x↔|y

SAY-OK-TO[RECIP]x↔|y

SAY-YES-TO[RECIP]x↔|y

Indicating verbs can be directed in space, which allows them to capitalize on the visual nature of ASL. This is used effectively when signers want to express the direction in which entities move or the location of an entity. For instance, depending on how you direct the sign THROW→L, you can demonstrate where an object has been directed. For instance,

THROW

THROW

Perhaps you are interested in expressing how you rearranged the furniture in your living room. Using an indicating verb allows you to demonstrate easily where an entity was moved from and to.

The chair is there. The table is there. Move the chair to the table.

MOVE ^{L1→L2}

In this example, the signer first sets the chair to her left and the table to her right. When she signs MOVE^{L1→L2}, she begins the sign on the left near the area associated with the chair and moves her hand to her right, ending near the area associated with the table. She is visually demonstrating where the chair originated in relation to the table, as well as the final location of the chair.

Locative verbs are another type of indicating verb. The location where such a verb is produced contributes to its meaning. The verb is produced at a specific location—for example, on the body—to produce a meaningful utterance. If you want to explain to someone about your recent shoulder surgery, the verb USE-SCALPEL would be articulated at your shoulder as opposed to your stomach.

Changes to an indicating verb's movement and location allow signers to show who is performing the action and who is at the receiving end of the action, or where the action took place. We will now move on to the final category of verbs in ASL.

Depicting Verbs

Depicting verbs are the most complex verb type in ASL. They are also arguably the most difficult for people learning ASL to master because of this complexity. Hopefully, by the end of this section, you will not only be impressed by the dynamics of depicting verbs, but you will also be eager to use them to more effectively express yourself in ASL.

Depicting verbs are unique in that they are able to convey two types of information simultaneously. The first piece of information expressed is that of their action or state of being. In addition to this, however, they depict certain aspects of their meaning. This duality is likely one of the reasons that learners struggle to master depicting verbs.

Depicting verbs can be divided into three subcategories. The first of these comprises depicting verbs that show where something is in space. We will refer to this category as the BE-AT depicting verbs. These verbs are used to give the topographical location of entities in space. They all share the same short, downward movement that ends with a pause at the topographical location of the entity. Here are several BE-AT depicting verbs:

Human being is at a location.

PERSON-BE-AT↓L1

Vehicle is at a location.

VEHICLE-BE-AT↓L1

A flat object is at a location (object such as a table, paper, and so on).

FLAT-ENTITY-BE-AT↓L1

Nonhuman entity is at a location.

ANIMAL-BE-AT↓L1

Signers use BE-AT verbs to place entities in a specific location. The entities are given an imagined area in the signing space, and this area of space is then associated with the entity.

A second category of depicting verbs is used to signify the shape and extent of a surface or the extent of a linear arrangement of entities. The formation of these depicting verbs differs from the BE-AT verbs in that both hands are typically involved; each hand has the same handshape, and one hand remains stationary while the other moves. However, in some cases, both hands retain the same handshape but move in either the same or opposite directions. Let's look at some examples of this type of depicting verb:

A flat surface that extends some distance (such as a lake)

FLAT-BROAD-SURFACE-EXTEND-TO ↓L1-L2

A bumpy surface that extends some distance (such as a road under construction)

BUMPY-BROAD-SURFACE-EXTEND-TO ↓L1-L2

A narrow, cylindrical object of some length (such as tubing)

SMALL-CYLINDRICAL-SURFACE-EXTEND-TO ↓L1-L2

A wide, cylindrical object of some length (such as pipe)

LARGE-CYLINDIRCAL-SURFACE-EXTEND-TO ↓L1-L2

These depicting verbs use the shape and movement of the hands to provide an approximate demonstration of the shape of the entity being described. I use the word *approximate* because the actual size of the entity being described might be significantly larger or smaller than the size of a signer's hands and longer or shorter than the distance he extends his arms. For instance, suppose a signer was describing a new highway that had just been laid. He would likely use the depicting verb FLAT-BROAD-SURFACE-EXTEND-TO ↓L1-L2 to describe the new surface, since it is smooth, flat, and extends for some distance. However, the same verb could be used in the description of a desert, which also has a flat surface that extends a great distance. A desert is a much larger scale entity than a highway. The depicting verb FLAT-BROAD-SURFACE-EXTEND-TO$^{\downarrow L1-L2}$ is not associated with a single entity; it is used to describe the physical nature of surfaces that have the characteristics of being flat and broad. Notice that in the articulation of these signs the non-manual signals are different.

It is also possible to use this second type of depicting verb to show the arrangement of entities. If you wanted to express a number of cars lined up in a row, perhaps at a car dealership, it would look like this:

VEHICLE-ROW-EXTEND-TO $^{\downarrow L1-L2}$

The depicting verb VEHICLE-ROW-EXTEND-TO$^{\downarrow L1-L2}$ provides a visual representation of how the cars were arranged. Again, the size of the actual entity has been compressed significantly. A signer's hand is much smaller than an actual automobile, and the distance between the stationary left hand and the moving right hand is also smaller than the physical space that a row of cars would require.

The final type of depicting verb is one that shows movements or actions. This type of verb not only shows the path in which an entity moves, it also can show the manner in which the movement occurs. You might want to express that you walked from one location to another. You could do so using a depicting verb such as this one:

UPRIGHT-PERSON-WALK-TO $^{\downarrow L1-L2}$

The signer produces a vertically oriented 1 handshape and moves the hand from her right to her left side while producing the verb UPRIGHT-PERSON-WALK-TO$^{\downarrow L1\text{-}L2}$. The palm-side surface of the finger corresponds to the front of the person walking. The signer could also produce the same verb to indicate moving in the opposite direction:

UPRIGHT-PERSON-WALK-TO $^{\downarrow L1\text{-}L2}$

This time she initiates the sign on her left side and moves her hand across her body to the right. This means "walking from point A to point B."

A signer could further alter the production of the UPRIGHT-PERSON-WALK-TO$^{\downarrow L1\text{-}L2}$ verb by adding a slight up-and-down movement at the same time the hand is moving across the body. This verb expresses a person walking in a leisurely manner between points A and B. Notice that the nonmanual signals in all three productions of the verb are different.

In all of these examples, we see that the depicting verb expresses not only the action, but also the manner in which the action takes place. This collapsing of two types of information into the verb is very different than what occurs in the English verb system. A single verb in English does not express the equivalent information. For instance, "The person walked backward." The adverb *backward* is needed to express the direction in which the person walked. The verb *walked* does not—nor can it be conjugated in any way to—express this information.

As you can see, the verb system in ASL is fascinating and has a structure quite dissimilar from that of English. While the languages are able to express equivalent concepts, the verb forms for doing so are very different. People often comment that the ASL lexicon is far smaller than that of English. In other words, if you compared the size of an ASL dictionary to that of an English dictionary, the latter would be thicker. This physical difference in the number of signs compared to the number of words is then interpreted as meaning that ASL's capacity for expressing concepts is more limited than that of English (or other spoken languages). This is, of course, false.

The problem with comparing the lexicons of the two languages is that the many ways a verb can be produced in ASL is often captured in a dictionary by a single citation form. Take the indicating verb GIVE, which was used in several examples throughout this chapter. In a dictionary, it is given a single entry in which the citation form is described and illustrated. While this is an accurate representation of the basic form, it does not accurately represent the ways in which it can be modified. Depicting verbs are even more elusive. Because their use is inseparably linked to the context in which they appear, they often do not even warrant a dictionary entry. Thus, a huge portion of ASL's lexicon is never captured on paper.

Becoming accustomed to the verb system in ASL requires practice. It is often difficult to get used to collapsing a concept that requires two, three, or more words in English into a single sign. As you use the language, however, you will begin to realize the effectiveness of the ASL verb system.

Chapter Summary

In this chapter, you were introduced to the verb system in ASL and learned the following:

1. ASL verbs are grouped according to how the sign is produced.

2. ASL has three types of verbs: plain, indicating, and depicting.

3. Plain verbs are produced in a static location. A change in the articulation of a plain verb will change it to another verb or result in ungrammatical usage.

4. Indicating verbs can be directed in space to provide additional information about the subject and/or object of the sentence.

5. Indicating verbs encode meaning about singular and plural objects.

6. Reciprocal verbs are a type of indicating verb and express two people performing the same action simultaneously. They are produced with both hands producing the same verb in opposite directions at the same time.

7. Locative verbs are a type of indicating verb. The location where the verb is articulated contributes information about the verb.

8. Depicting verbs convey two types of information simultaneously: the action or state of being, and an aspect of their meaning. There are three types of depicting verbs:

   a. BE-AT verbs that establish an entity at a location. They are formed with a short, downward movement and a hold.

   b. Depicting verbs that signify shape and extent of a surface or linear arrangement of entities. They are formed with two hands of the same handshape. One hand remains stationary, while the other moves.

   c. Depicting verbs showing movement or action and the manner of the movement or action. The form is dependent on the meaning being expressed.

9. There are conventions for writing signs that are directed or placed in signing space.

QUIZ

1. True or false: Plain verbs are a group of verbs that are produced in a static location, and the articulation of the sign cannot be altered.

2. Which of the following are plain verbs?

   (a) EAT

   (b) GIVE

   (c) FORGET

   (d) TELL

   (e) DREAM

   (f) ANSWER

3. True or false: Indicating verbs cannot be directed in space.

4. Which of the following are indicating verbs?

   (a) GIVE

   (b) FORGET

   (c) LAUGH

   (d) BITE

   (e) FORCE

   (f) FLAT-BROAD-SURFACE-EXTEND-TO [↓L1-L2]

5. True or false: Indicating verbs can be used to indicate the involvement of more than two entities in a situation.

6. True or false: Depicting verbs convey information about their action or state of being, and they also depict certain aspects of their meaning.

7. True or false: There are four types of depicting verbs.

8. True or false: One type of depicting verb, the BE-AT verb, is used to give the topographical location of entities in space.

9. True or false: Another type of depicting verb is one that shows movements or actions.

10. Which of the following are depicting verbs?

    (a) CALL-BY-PHONE[¬y]

    (b) PERSON-BE-AT[↓L1]

    (c) LOVE

    (d) LOOK-AT[¬y]

    (e) UPRIGHT-PERSON-WALK-TO[↓L1-L2]

    (f) SMALL-CYLINDRICAL-SURFACE-EXTEND-TO[↓L1-L2]

CHAPTER 5

Deaf Etiquette

It should be fair to assume if you are dedicating time to learning ASL that you are interested in using the language at some point. This means you will interact with deaf people or ASL users familiar with the Deaf community. In this chapter I would like to offer you some insight on the norms of behavior of Deaf people as well as differences between ASL users and English speakers.

Deaf Is Not a Four-Letter Word

It is important to recognize that people who are Deaf and use ASL consider themselves members of a cultural group separate from speakers of English. They share common experiences, beliefs, and most significantly, a language. Deaf people do not view themselves as disabled but rather as members of a linguistic minority. English speakers often avoid using the English word *deaf* when referring to Deaf people. They think it is impolite, preferring labels such as "hearing impaired" or "hard of hearing." Deaf people find this avoidance of the word interesting, because they do not have an aversion to the label—in fact, quite the opposite.

While speakers of English avoid the label *deaf*, they are often intrigued by knowing how much a Deaf person can hear or how the person became deaf. Deaf people do not find these things important and, as a matter of fact, never ask each other about them. One should avoid asking these questions of Deaf people. If the information is offered, that's fine, but it shouldn't be requested.

Introducing Yourself and Others

Initiating a conversation with a person you don't know is always a little intimidating. People develop conventions for introducing themselves and for making these initial contacts a bit smoother. What I will outline here are guidelines for the process of making introductions using the most common ways.

YOUR NAME

A logical starting point is to tell the other person what your name is. You will want to deliberately (in other words, clearly and slowly) finger spell your first and last name. (In Chapter 12, you will learn the manual alphabet.)

Name signs can be descriptive in that they incorporate a characteristic about the person (having long hair, smiling often, being tall, and so on). Other name signs are arbitrary, often using the first letter of a person's name. Here are some examples of what an introduction might look like:

My name is Barb.

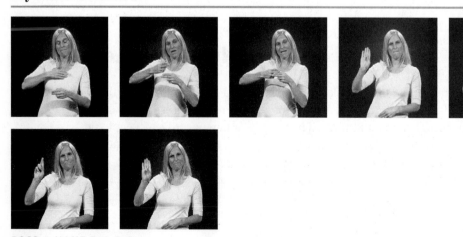

POSS-1 NAME B-A-R-B

My name is Carl.

POSS-1 NAME C-A-R-L

My name is Kerry.

POSS-1 NAME K-E-R-R-Y

The first two names, Barb and Carl, have arbitrary name signs that use the first letter of their names and a location, movement, and orientation to create a sign associated with each person. The last name sign, Kerry, uses a personal characteristic. Here, Kerry is known for smiling a lot, and this characteristic is incorporated into the name sign. Again, the first letter of the name is used, and a *k* is produced on the cheek.

You do not create your own name sign. Rather, one will be given to you by members of the Deaf community after you have socialized with them for a certain length of time. It will show that they no longer see you merely as a visitor but as someone who has begun to establish ties with the community. Until you have been given a name sign, your name will be finger spelled each time you are referenced.

Be aware that Deaf people do not know everyone's name sign, only those with whom they interact on a frequent basis. If you use a name sign with which someone is unfamiliar, you will want to provide the person's full first and last name. Also, knowing how to spell a person's name correctly is important.

YOUR BIOGRAPHY

Once you have exchanged full names and name signs, it is customary to provide a short history of yourself. When Deaf people meet other Deaf people, this biography includes the following information:

- Where they grew up (the state)

- Where they went to school (In the past, this meant identifying the residential school for the deaf they attended. Today, it can also include whether they attended a mainstream school or not.)

- Whether or not they have Deaf parents

You will use a similar template for your biography. The difference will be that you will not be expected to identify the school you attended. Instead, you should provide some information about why you are introducing yourself to the Deaf person, how you learned ASL, and how long you have been studying the language. This series of questions provides a basis for initiating further conversation and is useful in that it gives you a starting point from which to build.

You should follow the same process when introducing another person. This time, however, you will need to provide information about both people. You begin by producing their first and last names and their name signs, if appropriate. You then provide the short biographies about both individuals. The goal is to provide each person with background about the other so they can find some common connection on which to base a conversation.

In Chapter 7, you will learn the vocabulary for meeting and greeting people. There, I will explain additional rituals that can be followed for greeting and saying good-bye to people in ASL.

Appropriate Attention-Getting Techniques

There are several ways to get a Deaf person's attention. Which one you use will depend on the situation and circumstances. Just as you wouldn't yell in a library to get your friend's attention, you need to use judgment as to which method is most appropriate.

- **Flickering the lights.** One effective way of getting the attention of a large group of people—in a classroom, for instance—is to turn the overhead lights on and off repeatedly. This change in the visual environment signals to the group that there is information to be relayed. Flickering lights can be used in other settings as well. Deaf people connect their doorbells to indoor lighting, so when the doorbell is pressed, a light in the house will turn on and off.

- **Waving.** Another method of getting a Deaf person's attention is to wave your hand. The extent of this movement varies, depending on your proximity to the Deaf person. If you are sitting near the person, a small flexing and relaxing of the wrist may be enough, as shown here:

If, however, you are across the room from the person with whom you wish to interact, you will need to move your arm in a more pronounced way, with the entire arm becoming involved:

In this larger wave, you use the shoulder as opposed to the wrist to produce the movement. The speed with which you wave can also vary depending on the urgency with which you need (or want) to get the person's attention. If you start to wave frantically, you will give the impression that something is wrong.

- **Tapping.** Making physical contact with Deaf people by tapping them with your hand is an acceptable means of getting their attention. Contact is typically on the shoulder or arm. This method is used if you are in close proximity to a person. It also tends to be a method that people learning ASL are less comfortable using because English speakers are accustomed to far less physical contact when speaking than are ASL users when signing.

- **Foot stomping/hand pounding.** The final two common ways to get someone's attention is to either stomp your foot or pound on a hard surface with which the Deaf person is in contact. The purpose of these approaches is to cause vibrations or other movement that the person can feel. For this reason, the surface with which you make contact will influence whether or not it will be effective. Stomping on grass, for instance, will be less effective than stomping on a wood floor. Common sense should guide the use of hand pounding as well. You don't want to pound so hard on a table that you overturn beverages, for example. Look at these two methods on the DVD.

As with tapping, some people learning ASL are uncomfortable with pounding on a table. For English speakers, doing so usually indicates that someone is angry. ASL users do not have the same interpretation.

You Must Be Able to See

Once you have secured a person's attention, an effective interaction can occur only if you can see one another. This means you need to be aware of sight lines. Are there any physical obstructions between yourself and the person with whom you are attempting to converse? For instance, are you partially obstructed by a pole in the middle of the room? You will notice that ASL users often sit in circles or arcs to ensure that other people's bodies are not in the way.

Appropriate lighting is also important. Again, if you can't see the other person, you can't communicate. A semi-lit room may seem relaxing for an evening dinner, but if the room isn't bright enough, people's eyes begin to strain. Glare can be another problem. It may be necessary to draw the window blinds on a sunny day because there is a glare or a person sitting in front of the window is backlit, which makes seeing her—especially her face—difficult.

As I mentioned in Chapter 1, eye contact has a greater importance in ASL than in spoken English, because without it, a person will not receive the language. English speakers can look away while listening to another person. Sound waves are received by the ears regardless of where the eyes are directed. Not so with ASL. If eye contact is broken during an ASL conversation, the primary signer assumes that either there is a reason for the change in gaze, such as someone is interrupting the conversation, or the other person is no longer interested.

In other settings, eye contact must be managed to ensure that everyone has access to what is being signed. A classroom is one such setting in which eye gaze must be monitored. If a teacher is giving a lecture in ASL and students are taking notes on the lecture, it is critical that the teacher be aware that students will look down periodically. When they do, they are unable to receive additional input.

A situation sometimes arises that may seem to impact sight lines and the maintenance of eye contact. What do you do when two people are conversing in ASL and you need to pass between them? The short answer is walk between the signers with as little distraction as possible. Do not bend or crouch down and walk through; simply sign EXCUSE-ME and walk past. ASL signers will be able to monitor their interaction and repeat, if necessary, anything that may have been obstructed, but most likely, no information will have been lost. It is actually more distracting if you stand next to them, wait for them to notice you, explain that you need to pass, and wait for their acknowledgment to do so.

Personal Space

Personal space is defined as the area around individuals, which is reserved for themselves. This space is used for normal conversations. Every culture has different expectations about how small or large this area is. You may have had an experience in which you interacted with another person who had a different expectation of personal space. You may start a conversation and feel that the other person is too close, so you back up slightly until you feel there is a comfortable distance between you. The other person may now feel the distance is too great and move forward to decrease the space. This results in your discomfort, so you back up again. This personal space two-step may continue until the conversation ends or a physical obstruction prevents your continued retreat.

Users of ASL have their own expectations of what the default distance should be. It will vary slightly depending on the participants (whether the conversation is between close friends or new acquaintances) and the setting. Generally speaking, however, there are acceptable distances between signers. The distance between two signers needs to be far enough to allow for easy viewing of their hands, faces, and bodies. If signers are too close together, this is difficult. You can transmit ASL over greater distances than is possible with spoken English. The ability to see signs is greater than the ability to hear words. It is not likely that you will want to conduct a conversation across large expanses, but it is possible to have a limited exchange much more easily than with a spoken language. This difference is useful in a public space such as a restaurant, where it is not acceptable to yell across the room, but it would be possible to have a short exchange in ASL.

As mentioned in the section about attention-getting techniques, the ability to enter another's personal space is different in ASL than in English. It is acceptable to touch another signer in order to get his attention. English speakers typically make far less physical contact than do ASL signers.

Conversational Etiquette

Once you are fluent enough to have a conversation, you will need to learn to follow the expected ASL conventions. We have already discussed the importance of eye contact, but there are some additional interactional norms that will allow you to navigate a conversation more effectively.

The first is that those in an ASL conversation expect that you will give visual cues to show that you are attending to and/or understanding what is being signed. This type of feedback is called *back-channeling*, and it can happen in various ways. The most common is probably nodding or shaking your head. Nodding your head is generally used to show that you are following the conversation; however, shaking your head can signify that you disagree with what was just said or that you empathize with a problematic situation. This is a visual cue that you are attending to what the other person is signing and are engaged in the conversation.

Another back-channeling option is the use of a sign that is often glossed as OH-I-SEE, one version of which looks like this:

OH-I-SEE

This sign is produced with a slight repetition when it means "I am following what you are saying." Sometimes, however, you may be responding to information provided by the other signer to clarify or explain something you have been trying to understand. The production of the sign changes to convey the idea "I understand now" or "That explains it for me." This form of the sign OH-I-SEE looks like this:

OH-I-SEE

This version of the sign is produced with movement from the elbow and shoulder rather than just the wrist. The accompanying nonmanual signal is also different than in the first version. It is larger in its articulation because of the movement from the elbow and wrist rather than wrist only.

Learning how to interrupt or take a turn in an appropriate way is an important aspect of an ASL conversation. This may be easier to do in one-on-one conversation than in a group discussion. If you are having a conversation with one other person and she asks a question, you know you are expected to answer. In a situation in which several people are interacting, it can be more difficult to determine if you should answer or, if you and another person want to answer at the same time, who should answer first.

Generally speaking, you want to wait until the other person finishes signing before you start. However, you may want to raise your hands to indicate to the other signer that you are ready to make a contribution to the conversation. There may be situations in which you need to interrupt someone before he has finished, and it is acceptable to do so if the circumstances dictate. The phrase SORRY INTERRUPT is a polite way of accomplishing this:

SORRY INTERRUPT

The phrase SORRY INTERRUPT is then followed by whatever you needed to relay to the other person.

While having a conversation, be honest when you do not understand or need clarification. Native users of a language are often understanding and accommodating of a language learning curve for anyone learning that language. It is much more beneficial for you to admit that you need help understanding. Remember that Deaf people have a lot of experience interacting with non-ASL users. This means they are quite adept at making themselves understood. They will be more than happy to repeat themselves or restructure a sentence in a way that you will understand. Pretending to comprehend something when you don't will most likely result in a misunderstanding or an awkward moment when you have been asked a question but are unable to answer because you have been unable to follow the exchange.

To let the other person know you need clarification, you can use one of the following phrases:

I don't understand.

$$\overline{\text{PRO-1 NOT UNDERSTAND}}^{\text{neg}}$$

Could you please repeat yourself?

AGAIN PLEASE

What do you mean?

MEAN?

The first phrase,

$$\overline{\text{PRO-1 NOT UNDERSTAND}}^{\text{neg}}$$

means "I don't understand" and is the simplest way of conveying to the other signer that you are not following what she is signing. Another approach is to repeat the sign you don't understand followed by the sign MEAN. This is similar to asking, "What does *x* mean?" or "What do you mean?" Of course you can always rely on the "I'm lost" facial expression, and the signer will undoubtedly start again. The point is to request clarification as you need it.

You may also find that you need to correct something you have just signed. Perhaps you used the wrong sign or simply conveyed the wrong information. If so, you can use the following phrase:

I am mistaken. What I meant to say is . . .

PRO-1 WRONG PRO-1 MEAN

This signals to the other person that you mis-signed and are correcting what you just said.

Lipreading

Many people who use spoken English wonder why Deaf people don't just learn to lip-read. The short answer: because it is extremely difficult. The reason is that many sounds in English are not distinguishable based on what the lips do but on what happens inside the mouth and throat. Try this experiment. Go to a mirror and make the sounds / p / and / b /. Now produce the lip movements without the sound. What do you see? They look exactly the same. You know they are different letters because of the sound you make, not because of how your lips are shaped. The same is true for / t / and / d /, and / s / and / z /. Vowels are even more elusive since the sounds are made almost entirely within the mouth. It has been estimated that only 30 to 40 percent of the sounds in English are distinguishable by sight alone. This leaves a lot of room for misunderstanding. Have you ever been in your car with the windows rolled up and had someone come over to tell you something? What is the first thing you do? Roll down the window! If lipreading were easy, you wouldn't need to have the window down to understand the other person.

Some Deaf people are able to figure out simple English sentences when they are spoken. This is often based on the context provided by a situation, such as "Can you lip-read?" or "What time is it?" This does not mean that the person wants or is able to have an entire conversation relying only on lipreading. If in the course of a conversation you come to an impasse and can't express yourself using ASL, it will be more effective to write down what you are trying to convey rather than simply saying it and expecting the Deaf person to read your lips.

Use of Physical Descriptions

Some English speakers find that Deaf people are more direct than they are accustomed to. One reason is that Deaf people rely on physical appearances to identify people. They may state the following when identifying someone:

MAN THERE LARGE

The utterance

MAN THERE LARGE

means "See the large man over there." The fact that the signer draws attention to the other person's size or weight would be considered indiscreet by many English speakers. In ASL, however, it is permissible to use such physical characteristics to identify people. Due to the visual nature of the language, visual cues are often paramount when describing people. It is common for ASL users to make comments about physical changes in people whom they have not seen in a long time. Deaf people often explain that they make such comments because the deaf community is a very small and tight-knit group; therefore, their comments or questions may appear to be more intimate.

Chapter Summary

The goal of this chapter was to give you some insights into the behaviors and social norms of deaf people. In this chapter, you learned the following:

1. That Deaf people are members of a separate culture that is connected by a common language (ASL) and common experiences, traditions, and beliefs. Viewing Deaf people as a distinct cultural group will help you better understand their experiences.

2. How to introduce yourself and others in ASL, as well as what name signs are.

3. Appropriate ways of getting a Deaf person's attention, including flickering lights, waving your hand or arm, tapping the person on the shoulder or arm, foot stomping, and hand pounding.

4. The importance of sight lines and appropriately lit spaces.

5. What is considered appropriate personal space in ASL conversations.

6. The importance of providing back-channeling in an ASL conversation and ways of doing so, such as head nodding and signing OH-I-SEE.

7. How to interrupt an ASL conversation using SORRY INTERRUPT.

8. The importance of admitting when you do not understand something or need clarification using phrases such as

$$\overline{\text{PRO-1 NOT UNDERSTAND}}^{\text{neg}}$$

and AGAIN PLEASE.

9. How to correct yourself (PRO-1 WRONG PRO-1 MEAN) when you have mis-signed or provided incorrect information.

10. That Deaf people avoid relying on lipreading English because 60 to 70 percent of English sounds are not distinguishable based on lip movements.

11. That Deaf people tend to rely on physical characteristics to identify people.

QUIZ

1. True or false: Deaf people avoid using the label *deaf* to describe themselves.

2. True or false: Name signs are signs used as people's names to avoid finger spelling a name every time it is used.

3. True or false: Flickering lights is not an acceptable way of getting the attention of a large group of Deaf people.

4. True or false: Tapping a Deaf person is an acceptable means of getting that person's attention.

5. True or false: Stomping your foot is an acceptable means of getting a Deaf person's attention.

6. True or false: Being able to see a person clearly is unnecessary when using ASL.

7. True or false: Back-channeling in ASL means providing visual cues that indicate you are attending to and/or understanding what is being signed.

8. True or false: The sign OH-I-SEE is a back-channeling option in ASL.

9. True or false: Lipreading is an effective way for all Deaf people to understand English speakers.

10. True or false: ASL users avoid the use of physical descriptions when identifying people to one another.

CHAPTER 6

Variation in ASL

"Where is the bubbler?" "Do you want a cabinet?" I was asked these two questions shortly after the start of my fall semester freshman year at an East Coast university. My response to both questions was a blank face. I had absolutely no idea how to respond. The reason for my confusion was that I had grown up in the Midwest and was unfamiliar with the use of the words *bubbler* and *cabinet* in the context used here. In Rhode Island, *bubbler* refers to a water fountain, and a *cabinet* is a milk shake. Differences in the labels given to the same item in the same language is called *variation*. All languages exhibit variation, and ASL is no exception.

This chapter will introduce you to the concept of language variation. I will illustrate different types of variation that are seen in ASL, as well as reasons that contribute to the existence of variation.

I believe it is important for any language learner to have some understanding of variation, because it can often be a source of confusion in a new language. Once a student leaves the classroom (or book) and attempts to interact with native users of the language, he is frustrated by the fact that what people do is different than what he learned in the formal setting. There are several reasons for this difference, but one important reason is that language varies. How people use a language with their friends is different than how they use it in the work environment. Lexical items for people who grew up in the Midwest differ from those who grew up in other parts of the country. These variations exist, and if you become aware of them as you are learning the language, some (although not all!) of the confusion and frustration will be mitigated.

What Is Language Variation?

Language variation refers to the different ways people have of expressing the same thing. In English, for example, we may use the words *pop*, *soda*, *Coke*, *tonic*, *soda pop*, and *soft drink* to refer to the same carbonated beverage. In ASL, the sign that expresses the concept "birthday" can be signed in the following ways:

BIRTHDAY   BIRTHDAY   BIRTHDAY

Most of the time variation does not hinder communication between speakers of the same language. When English speakers from the Midwest travel to the East Coast, they have little trouble adjusting to the terminology of the new location and will order a "soda" rather than a "pop." The preceding photos are examples of *lexical variation*, which means that different lexical items are semantically the same.

Another difference that speakers of English notice if they travel throughout the United States is that people pronounce words differently. An example of this is how many people from Rhode Island pronounce words that end in the vowel sound / a /. English speakers from Rhode Island will replace the / a / with / -er /. The result is words such as *visa*, *Linda*, and *Lisa* being pronounced "viser," "Linder," and "Liser." How vowels are pronounced in the United States varies widely. Say the following words to yourself: *dawn* and *Don*, *cot* and *caught*, *pin* and *pen*, *Mary* and *merry*, *hawk* and *hock*. When you pronounce them, do they sound the same? Some American English speakers pronounce the vowels in each pair distinctly, whereas others say them with the same sounds. This difference in pronunciation is called *accent*. Although we often to refer to people whose manner of pronunciation differs from our own as "having an accent," the reality is that everyone has an accent.

There are also instances in which the structure of the sentence is different depending on the speaker. Suppose you go to get lunch at a local deli. It will likely be busy, and you will have to wait your turn to order. In the United States, we have the convention of standing with one person behind the next. As the first person completes her order, the person behind her moves forward for his turn. How people describe this can vary depending on where in the United States they are from; some speakers say the people are "standing *in* line," while others say "standing *on* line."

When there is a difference in the pronunciation, vocabulary, or syntax of a language, we call this variation a *dialect*. Dialects of a language are usually spoken by a group united by geography or social status.

With this background in language variation, you can now learn about how ASL varies.

Types of Variation in ASL

In the preceding section, you learned that languages can vary phonologically, morphologically, and syntactically. ASL exhibits the same types of variation. Let's look at examples of each.

PHONOLOGICAL VARIATION IN ASL

Recall what you learned about the formation of individual signs in ASL. They can be divided into postures and transitions. Three linguistic features—the handshape, the placement hand, and the orientation of the hand—can describe each posture. Changes to any of these features can alter the "pronunciation" of the sign.

Let's first look at differences in the handshapes used to produce variants of a sign.

FUNNY   **COMPUTER**

The signs FUNNY and COMPUTER illustrate how a sign can vary with a change in the handshape used. The differences in the handshape can be subtle, as in the thumb extension or bend in the sign FUNNY, or more noticeable, as in the different handshapes used in the sign COMPUTER. (See the DVD for variants of COP, BANANA, and PRO-1.)

It is possible to change the placement of a sign. Location refers to where the sign is produced, sometimes called the placement. For example, in the production of KNOW, the location of where the sign is made changes:

KNOW

(See the DVD for FOR, SUPPOSE, and SEARCH.)

Another way location can change is when the places where the sign starts and ends are exchanged in the same sign. This is called *metathesis*. Here is an example of signs that vary in this way:

DEAF   **RESTAURANT**

When producing the signs DEAF or RESTAURANT, the locations where the signs begin and end can be reversed.

A third feature that can change is the orientation of the hand when the sign is made. This difference can be seen in a variation of the sign COP:

COP

The signer can articulate the sign COP with the palm directed to the side or toward the body.

A number of signs in ASL are produced with two hands that do the same thing on opposite sides of the body. Oftentimes, these two-handed signs are produced with only one hand, dropping what is essentially redundant information. When a signer produces YOUNG, for example, she may use two hands or one.

YOUNG

Phonological differences in how signs are produced parallel the differences in how English speakers pronounce individual sounds.

LEXICAL VARIATION

Sometimes two completely different lexical signs refer to the same concept or entity. Instead of a change of a single feature of a posture, the sign is created completely differently. Here are several examples (see also examples on the DVD):

COMPUTER   **JAPAN**

DEAF

These examples provide a sampling of different lexical signs that refer to the same concept or entity. Initially it may be confusing if someone uses a sign you are not familiar with. My advice is to consider the context in which it is used to help you figure out the meaning. If you are still unable to understand, ask the other person. Deaf signers themselves often encounter signs they have never seen because the sign is unique to a particular region of the country or social group.

SYNTACTIC VARIATION IN ASL

How signs are arranged in a sentence can also vary. There are more limited examples of this, because it has not been studied a lot and it is more difficult to determine whether two sentences convey the same meaning. Despite this, there is evidence that use of PRO-1 and PRO$^{\rightarrow x}$ in sentences seems to vary. For instance, if a signer is expressing that she gave something to someone else, she could produce the following sentences:

PRO-1 GIVE PRO$^{\rightarrow x}$

GIVE PRO$^{\rightarrow x}$

GIVE

In these three examples, the signer can overtly produce the first and non–first person pronouns (PRO-1 and PRO^{-x}) or omit one or both of them because the indicating verb GIVE is directed toward token spaces or entities present that are associated with the giver and recipient, making the use of PRO-1 and PRO^{-x} unnecessary. This same variation occurs for plain verbs.

Reasons for Variation

Now that you have been to exposed to variations in ASL, you may be wondering why this happens. Let's look at what contributes to the existence of variation.

LINGUISTIC REASONS

One factor that impacts how a sign is produced is where the sign occurs in relation to other signs. Linguists sometimes refer to this as the *linguistic environment*. Signs are not produced in isolation but are strung together. Which sign comes before or after another sign can affect how the middle sign is produced. Let's look at some examples of this:

GIRL FUNNY

The citation form of FUNNY looks like this:

FUNNY

In the preceding above, the signer's thumb is extended (sticks out to the side). This is likely because the sign before FUNNY is GIRL, in which the thumb is

extended. It is easier for the signer to simply extend the pointer and middle finger to produce the sign FUNNY rather than extend the two fingers and bend the thumb in. This change in how the handshape is made is called *handshape assimilation*. The second handshape assimilates, or looks like, the first.

The location where a sign is produced can have a similar influence on the surrounding signs. Compare the location of where KNOW is produced in the following two examples:

PRO⁻ˣ KNOW

FATHER KNOW

In the example PRO⁻ˣ KNOW, the signer produces the sign KNOW on her cheek. However, when she signs FATHER KNOW, KNOW is produced at her forehead. The reason is the locations of the preceding signs. PRO⁻ˣ is produced lower in the signing space, at the level of her chest. FATHER is made higher in the signing space, in the middle of her forehead. It is physically more efficient to produce the sign KNOW closer to the location of the previous sign. This results in KNOW being produced in a non–citation form location in PRO⁻ˣ KNOW, at her cheek.

English speakers change the way they pronounce words depending the environment. For instance, the sound / d / changes to / b / before words beginning with the sounds / m /, / b /, or / p /. Say the following phrases and notice what happens to the / d / sound: "bad pain," "blood pressure," "good morning," "old man." Did you pronounce the final sound in the first word? Of course, if you say the phrases carefully, you are able to articulate the final / d / sound, but more often than not in everyday speech, it merges with the first sound in the following word. When people hear these phrases, they have no trouble understanding what is being said. Similarly,

ASL users easily process what is being signed despite the slight variation in the production of individual signs.

A second reason that signs vary is the type of discourse in which they are produced. Was the signer having a conversation with a close friend, or was he giving a presentation for a group of people? The setting in which a person is signing can influence what lexical signs he uses, as well as how he articulates them.

Generally speaking, the more formal the discourse environment (such as a lecture or job interview), the more careful the sign production. The first effect of this is that signers are less likely to alter the production of signs (meaning less phonological variation). For example, two-handed signs, such as DEER, are produced with two hands. The second effect is the choice of signs that are used.

SOCIAL REASONS

In addition to linguistic influences, language also varies because of the social characteristics of the user. These social characteristics include geographic location, gender, age, ethnicity, and socioeconomic class, among others. Let's look at how social factors impact variation in ASL.

The first social characteristic we will examine is the geographic region where a signer lives. The most noticeable difference when you meet ASL users from different states is that there is a lot of lexical variation in their language. For example, there are several variations of COMPUTER. Depending on where you are in the country, you are more likely to see one variant over another.

In addition to lexical sign differences, other phonological differences between how people from different regions of the United States sign have been noted by researchers. Those from New York City are described as signing with greater speed than people from other states.

Another social factor is ethnicity. Differences between lexical signs of black ASL users and white ASL users have been documented. Compare the signs for TOMATO and PREGNANT.

TOMATO (white version)   **TOMATO (black version)**

PREGNANT (white version)   PREGNANT (black version)

As you can see, each group has different lexical signs for the same concepts. The differences in ethnic signing is a consequence of segregation of deaf schools in the South.

A third social factor that contributes to variation in ASL is gender. Men and women sign differently. The differences are phonological (how the individual signs are produced), as well as lexical (what signs men or women will use).

We will begin by looking at the differences in how men and women produce signs. One difference is that men typically produce signs lower than women. This is most evident when you look at signs that are produced in front of the body. Men tend to keep the elbows in a less flexed position, which results in the hands being lower, parallel with the chest and abdomen. Women, in contrast, tend to bend the elbows more, which means the hands are higher, parallel with the upper chest and neck. Further, men are described by ASL users as producing "larger" signs than women. This perception is based on the fact that men typically extend the arms more during sign production as compared to women. The following figure provides diagrams of how men and women produce signs as well as the extent of the signing area.

Look at the following examples of differences between male and female signers:

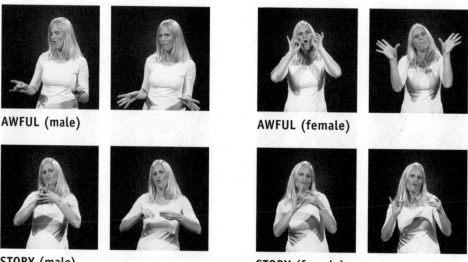

AWFUL (male)   AWFUL (female)

STORY (male)   STORY (female)

You can see that in the male version of AWFUL, the arm is more extended and the hand is directed downward. In the female version, the elbow is bent and the sign is directed upward. With the sign STORY, men are more likely to use a handshape in which all the fingers are used, while women tend to produce the sign with a single finger.

AGE OF ACQUISITION

A fourth social factor contributing to variation in ASL is the age at which a person learns the language. While it is difficult to determine the exact number, studies suggest that only about 10 percent of Deaf children have Deaf parents. This means that a majority of ASL users were not exposed to the language from birth, but at some point after that. This delay in exposure results in some signers not having native ASL skills. When a person begins learning ASL can affect his level of fluency.

Historical Change

One last matter should be discussed before we leave the topic of variation: historical change. All languages change over time. These changes can most easily be seen in changes to a language's vocabulary. Did anyone use the English words *e-mail* or *fax* prior to the 1980s? Or how about the question "Why don't you Google it and find out?"

ASL has changed over nearly two hundred years and will continue to do so. Let's look at some of these changes, beginning with those of lexical signs.

A number of signs have changed as the entities to which they refer have changed. For example, the sign TELEPHONE has changed as the technology has changed. Compare the old and new versions:

TELEPHONE
(old version)

TELEPHONE
(new version)

As you can see, the sign itself changed as the object changed. One of the most significant changes to vocabulary comes from signs that refer to new technology.

How signs are made also change over time. Some signs become more centralized, which means the location where they are produced moves closer to the center of a person's visual center. Here are some signs that have changed:

HELP (old version)   HELP (new version)

WILL (old version)   WILL (new version)

Both of these signs are now produced in a more centralized visual field, making them easier to see. In addition, the signs are easier to produce because the signer does not have to move the arms as far to make them.

Many signs that are produced with two hands had different handshapes on either hand that over time have become assimilated, or the same. The sign TOMATO is an example of this:

TOMATO   TOMATO

As with signs that have become more centralized, using the same handshapes for both hands makes the production of the sign easier. This is similar to how English speakers move to streamline words. The word *facsimile* was shortened to *fax*, and *electronic mail* quickly became *e-mail* because the latter terms were easier to say.

Chapter Summary

I have attempted to expose you to the variation you will encounter when you begin to use ASL in the deaf community. Being aware that people sign differently depending on the situation and their background will make the transition from classroom (or book) use of ASL to the real world a bit less daunting. One reason languages vary is because they are reflections of each person's individual identity. A common misconception of people who are unfamiliar with ASL about ASL users is the assumption that they are all the same. There is as much variety in ASL signers as in English speakers. The variation found in ASL is one reflection of this variety.

In this chapter, you learned the following:

1. Language variation means that people have different ways of saying the same thing.
2. ASL exhibits phonological, morphological, and syntactic variation.
3. The linguistic reasons ASL varies are the environment and the type of discourse in which the signing occurs.
4. The social reasons ASL varies include regional differences, ethnic differences, gender differences, and age of acquisition.
5. Languages change over time.
6. ASL signs have changed over time in the following ways: vocabulary changes, more centralized signs, and the assimilation of handshapes in two-handed signs.

QUIZ

1. The fact that languages can express the same concepts in different ways is referred to as what?
2. In English, a carbonated beverage can be referred to as *pop, soda, tonic, Coke,* or *soft drink.* This is an example of what type of variation?
3. If speakers of a language vary in pronunciation, vocabulary, and syntax, they are using a different _____.
4. True or false: ASL exhibits examples of phonological, morphological, and syntactic variation.
5. True or false: When the location where a sign starts and ends can be reversed, it is called metathesis.

6. True or false: These two signs for JAPAN show phonological variation in ASL.

7. True or false: The linguistic environment surrounding a sign can contribute to variation.

8. True or false: The type of discourse in which signs are used (a lecture versus a family dinner) does not cause variation in ASL.

9. True or false: One reason languages vary is because of social factors such as age, gender, and socioeconomic background.

10. True or false: Signs in ASL have not changed over the past hundred years.

CHAPTER 7

Meeting, Greeting, and Good-Byes

In the first six chapters, I provided you with some background about ASL and the deaf community. You are probably anxious to learn some signs so that you can start to interact with other ASL users. The subsequent chapters have been organized by topic and combine both sentences and vocabulary. The idea is that you can learn some basic sentences and then modify them as needed.

This chapter focuses on meeting and greeting people as well as saying good-bye.

Meeting and Greeting

As discussed in Chapter 5, a number of established questions are asked when you first meet someone. In this section, you will learn how to sign these questions, as well as how to respond.

Saying hello is simple. You can wave your hand as you do with English speakers:

The following is a slightly more formal way of greeting someone:

HELLO

If you are meeting someone for the first time you will likely exchange biographical information about yourselves beginning with your names.

What is your name?

POSS→ˣ NAME WHAT

My name is Sarah.

POSS-1 NAME S-A-R-A-H

My name sign is . . .

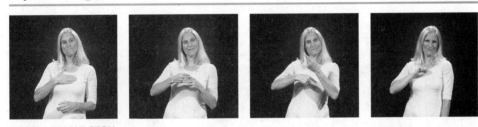

POSS-1 NAME SIGN

In more formal situations, such as when you introduce yourself or someone else before a lecture, you may see the following signs.

My name is Sarah Smith. (formal form)

I AM S-A-R-A-H S-M-I-T-H

This is Larry Smith. (formal form)

THIS IS L-A-R-R-Y S-M-I-T-H

Nice to meet you.

NICE MEET PRO→ˣ

Once you have learned each other's names, you may use a combination of the following questions and responses in your exchange:

How are you?

HOW PRO→ˣ

Possible responses to this question are as follows:

Fine.

FINE

Good.

GOOD

OK.

#O-K

What's up?

WHAT-UP

This phrase is used in more casual settings, typically with people with whom you are familiar.

I have not seen you in a long time.

PRO-1 NOT SEE PRO→ˣ UP-TILL-NOW

What have you been up to?

DO-DO UP-TIL-NOW

The same old routine.

SAME SAME

Once these pleasantries have been exchanged, you will want to return to gathering biographical information if you are conversing with someone you have just met.

Where do you live?

LIVE WHERE

Your response to this question will depend on the context of your conversation. Generally speaking, you start with the most general response and provide more detailed information if it is requested.

Begin with the name of your state. All fifty states are signed on the DVD, and you will see that some states have signs to represent them. For others, you finger spell part of the state name, and for a few others, you simply use the state's postal code abbreviation. A number of cities have specific signs as well. If the other person is familiar with your state, he may follow up with a question about which city you live in:

What city?

WHICH CITY

The DVD contains signs for the largest cities in the United States, including Atlanta, Baltimore, Boston, Buffalo, Chicago, Dallas, Denver, Houston, Los Angeles, New Orleans, New York City, Philadelphia, Pittsburgh, and St. Paul. For others, you will need to finger spell the name of the city.

Here is some additional vocabulary related to where you live:

City

CITY

Address

ADDRESS

How long have you lived there?

LIVE X HOW-LONG

People are also interested in knowing where you grew up.

Where did you grow up?

GROW UP WHERE

Here, you can identify the state and city. If you have lived in more than one place, you can list them. You can also sign the following:

I moved around a lot.

MOVE MOVE MOVE MOVE

You can expect to be asked whether you are Deaf or hearing, as well as whether or not your parents (or other family members) are Deaf. You may see one of the following questions:

Are you hearing?

PRO$^{\rightarrow X}$ HEARING

Are you Deaf?

PRO→X DEAF

Are you Deaf or hearing?

PRO→X DEAF HEARING WHICH

The following are possible responses to these questions:

I am hearing.

PRO-1 HEARING

I am Deaf.

PRO-1 DEAF

I am hard of hearing.

PRO-1 HARD-OF-HEARING

Are your parents Deaf?

POSS→X PARENTS DEAF

Is anyone else in your family Deaf?

ANYONE POSS→X FAMILY DEAF

One reason people ask about whether your parents or other family members are deaf is because they are interested in figuring out why you know ASL. If you respond that your parents are hearing, the person will likely follow up with a question such as this:

Where did you learn ASL?

PRO→ˣ LEARN ASL WHERE

To respond, you will want to identify where you learned signing. This may be the name of a school or university, or you may explain that you are self-taught. This information helps people determine your skill level and what level of fluency they can expect.

School

SCHOOL

University

UNIVERSITY

I taught myself.

TEACH SELF

Once you have been studying ASL, the following questions may be posed:

How long have you been studying ASL?

PRO→ˣ LEARN ASL HOW-LONG

To respond to this question, you will want to identify the appropriate period of time in months, years, and so on. You will learn more about time in Chapter 13.

Once the background has been established, the conversation will typically turn to more current biographical information such as the following:

Where do you work?

PRO^{→X} WORK WHERE

What do you do? What is your job?

POSS^{→X} #JOB DO-DO

If you are employed, you can respond with the name of your profession, such as the following:

Doctor

DOCTOR

Lawyer

LAWYER

Teacher/professor

TEACHER

Nurse

NURSE

See the DVD for the signs for other professions, including librarian, accountant, engineer, author/writer, actor, artist, information technology specialist, interpreter, boss, assistant, manager, supervisor, pilot, cop, principal, and president.

If you are a student, the following vocabulary is useful:

Student

STUDENT

Undergraduate

UNDERGRADUATE

Freshman

FRESHMAN

Sophomore

SOPHOMORE

Junior

JUNIOR

Senior

SENIOR

Graduate student

GRADUATE STUDENT

Finally, here are some additional questions you may be asked:

Are you married?

PRO→X MARRY

Are you single?

PRO→X SINGLE

Are you divorced?

PRO→X DIVORCE

Do you have children?

PRO→ˣ HAVE CHILDREN

Departing

When you are finished with a conversation, you will want to close with some pleasantries, such as these:

It was nice talking with you.

NICE CHAT

See you soon.

SEE PRO→ˣ SOON

Take care of yourself.

TAKE-CARE

Then you can close with a simple wave. It is important to note that good-byes between users of ASL may be more protracted than for English speakers. One important reason is that so few people know ASL, as compared to spoken English, that users are more reticent for the opportunity to converse with another person to end. You may also notice that when Deaf people turn and leave another Deaf person, they will often look back to make sure the other person doesn't have anything additional they want to add.

Chapter Summary

In this chapter, you learned:

1. How to say hello and greet people with initial pleasantries.
2. How to exchange biographical information, including
   (a) Your name and/or name sign
   (b) Where you live—city and state
   (c) Where you grew up
   (d) Whether you are hearing or deaf
   (e) Whether you have any family members who are deaf
   (f) Where you learned ASL and how long you have been studying the language
   (g) What your occupation is
   (h) Marital status
3. How to end a conversation and say good-bye.

QUIZ

All the sentences used in this quiz can be viewed on the DVD. You will need to view the sentences being signed in order to answer the questions.

1. What is the signer asking?
2. What did the signer say?
3. How could you respond to the signer's question?
4. What is the signer asking?
5. Respond to the signer's question in #4.
6. What is the signer asking?
7. Respond to the signer's question in #6.
8. What is the signer asking?
9. What is the signer asking?
10. Respond to the signer's question in #9.

CHAPTER 8

Asking Questions

In this chapter, you will learn how to ask questions in ASL. In Chapter 2, you were introduced to the importance of using your facial expressions to produce grammatically correct ASL. Then, in Chapter 3, you learned how these facial expressions, or nonmanual signals (NMSs), are used to identify different basic sentence structures. You were introduced to the different nonmanual signals used for yes/no questions and WH- questions.

In this chapter, we will review the nonmanual signals for those two types of questions and learn more about them. In addition, you will learn about a third type of question that is used in ASL: the rhetorical question.

Yes/No Questions

One type of question used in ASL is one that can be answered with either a *yes* or a *no*. For instance, the English question "Are you tired?"

To produce this type of question in ASL, you need to use a "yes/no" nonmanual signal. The NMS is used throughout the production of the sentence. (You will see when you learn about rhetorical questions that the nonmanual signal sometimes occurs with a single lexical sign.) To produce the yes/no NMS, the eyebrows are raised and the eyes may be widened. Let's look at an example:

The ASL sentence

$$\overline{\text{PRO}^{\rightarrow X}\ \text{TIRED}}^{\ y/n}$$

is how you would ask the English question "Are you tired?" The signer's eyebrows are raised and her eyes are slightly widened as she simultaneously produces the signs PRO$^{\rightarrow x}$ and TIRED.

Let's look at several more examples to give you additional practice with the yes/no question. The English question is given first, followed by how it would be asked in ASL.

Are you going?

PRO$^{\rightarrow X}$ GO

Are you cold?

PRO$^{\rightarrow X}$ COLD

Is Mom here?

MOM HERE

Can I join you?

CAN PRO-1 JOIN

Here is an alternate way of asking the same question. This one assumes the subject (you) and the object (the person you are asking) are both known.

CAN JOIN

Do you like school?

PRO→X LIKE SCHOOL

Are you hungry?

PRO→ˣ HUNGRY

As you can see, you can ask many yes/no questions once you know the correct nonmanual signal to use and how to use it.

WH- Questions

While yes/no questions are useful, the answers you will get are limited to either positive or negative responses. To ask questions that will elicit more informative responses, you will want to use WH- questions. These are questions that often involve the following lexical signs:

Who

WHO

What

WHAT   WHAT

The second version of the WHAT sign is less commonly used now, but you may still see it.

When

WHEN

Where

WHERE

Why

WHY

WHY

How

HOW

Which

WHICH

WH- questions require a response other than *yes* or *no*. To ask this type of question, your sentence will often use one of the six signs listed but will always use the WH- question nonmanual signal in which the eyebrows are furrowed, pointing downward. Here is an example of how to ask "What is your name?" in ASL:

POSS→ˣ NAME WHAT

As with a yes/no question, the NMS is produced simultaneously with the signs. Here are several examples of WH- questions. They are divided by the lexical signs they use.

WHAT

What do you want?

PRO→ˣ WANT WHAT

What is your favorite food?

POSS→X FAVORITE FOOD WHAT

WHO

Who is our teacher?

POSS-1 TEACHER WHO

Who is that person?

PERSON THERE WHO

WHEN

When do you leave?

PRO→ˣ LEAVE WHEN

When is summer vacation?

SUMMER VACATION WHEN

WHERE

Where do you live?

PRO→ˣ LIVE WHERE

Where is the book?

BOOK WHERE

WHY

Why are you leaving early?

PRO→ˣ LEAVE EARLY WHY

Why are you upset?

PRO→ˣ UPSET WHY

HOW

How do you know each other?

PRO→ˣ KNOW EACH-OTHER HOW

How did you learn ASL?

PRO→ˣ LEARN ASL HOW

To express the concepts of "how much" or "how many," ASL has a separate lexical sign that looks like this:

HOW-MANY

This sign is accompanied by the same nonmanual signal as the other lexical signs used in WH- questions. Here is an example:

How many people are in your family?

HOW-MANY PEOPLE POSS—ˣ FAMILY

To express the concept "how long," ASL uses the following sign:

HOW-LONG

It is also produced with the WH- question nonmanual signal, as in this example:

How long have you lived here?

PRO→ˣ LIVE HERE HOW-LONG

WHICH

Do you prefer to play volleyball or basketball?

PRO→ˣ PREFER PLAY VOLLEYBALL BASKETBALL WHICH

Do you use a MAC or a PC?

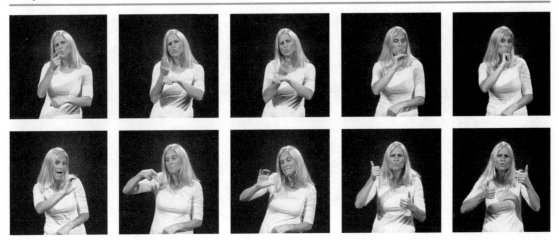

PRO→ˣ **USE M-A-C P-C WHICH**

Now that you are familiar with WH- questions and sentences produced with this construction, I will complicate matters a little. WH- questions do not always have a WH- lexical sign in them. This is because the nonmanual signal is enough to signal that a question is being asked. WH- questions that do not contain the lexical signs WHO, WHAT, WHEN, WHERE, WHY, HOW, or WHICH often confuse people new to ASL who rely on these signs to signal a question rather than attending to the signer's face for the NMS. Look at the following examples of WH- questions:

What is your name?

NAME POSS→ˣ

What color are your socks?

POSS→ˣ SOCKS COLOR

See how the face alone can signal that a question is being asked.

Rhetorical Questions

"How many times do I have to tell you not to come in the house with mud on your shoes?" If your mother asks you this question, you know she is not expecting you to give her an answer. In fact, doing so will likely make the situation worse. This is an example of a rhetorical question. Rhetorical questions are asked without the expectation of getting a response from the person with whom you are conversing. The use of rhetorical questions in spoken English is less frequent than in ASL; such questions allow a signer to emphasize a specific idea or point in the sentence, as in this example:

PRO→ˣ HAPPY WHY SUMMER VACATION

This sentence means "She is happy because it is summer vacation." Notice that when the signer produces the sign WHY, her eyebrows are raised and her head tilted slightly back; this is the nonmanual signal that accompanies a rhetorical question. Unlike yes/no and WH- questions, the NMS occurs during the production of a single lexical sign rather than throughout the entire sentence. The signer's facial expression is neutral as she signs PRO→ˣ HAPPY, then when she signs WHY, she adds the rhetorical question nonmanual signal. Her facial expression returns to neutral as she signs SUMMER VACATION.

Here are some additional examples of rhetorical questions:

He is upset because he lost.

PRO→ˣ UPSET WHY PRO→ˣ LOST

I am exhausted because I was up all night studying.

PRO-1 TIRED WHY PRO→ˣ STUDY ALL-NIGHT

A word of caution about the rhetorical question construction. Although it is used more frequently in ASL than in spoken English, it isn't used all the time. It is more typical of instructional situations (in the classroom, lectures, interactions with young children). People learning ASL often start to use rhetorical questions all the time once they learn how, but you should only use them when you want to emphasize a point. Don't go overboard.

Question Mark Wiggle

ASL has another lexical sign often referred to as the *question mark wiggle*, and it looks like this:

QM

This sign is added to questions in which the signer is surprised by information he has just been given. Suppose a classmate remarks on how easy your physics final exam was—a test you thought was quite challenging. You could respond with the following:

PRO→ˣ THINK TEST EASY QM

The sentence is produced with a nonmanual signal of raising the eyebrows as well as leaning the body slightly forward.

Chapter Summary

In this chapter, I showed you ways to ask questions in ASL and that the use of non-manual signals is important in producing grammatically correct questions. You learned about the following:

1. Yes/no questions. These questions elicit a response of either *yes* or *no*. They are produced with a nonmanual signal of raised eyebrows.

2. WH- questions. These questions bring you responses with more information. They are produced with a nonmanual signal of furrowed or downward-directed eyebrows.

3. Rhetorical questions. These questions are asked without the expectation of a response from the other person. They are used to draw attention to or emphasize one point in the sentence. The raised eyebrows NMS is produced only with the question lexical sign.

4. Question mark wiggle. This lexical sign is added to the end of a question used in response to something the signer has just been told but is surprised about.

QUIZ

All the sentences used in this quiz can be viewed on the DVD. You will need to view the sentences being signed in order to answer the questions.

1. What type of question is the signer asking (yes/no, WH-, rhetorical, question mark wiggle)?

2. What type of question is the signer asking (yes/no, WH-, rhetorical, question mark wiggle)?

3. What type of question is the signer asking (yes/no, WH-, rhetorical, question mark wiggle)?

4. What type of question is the signer asking (yes/no, WH-, rhetorical, question mark wiggle)?

5. What type of question is the signer asking (yes/no, WH-, rhetorical, question mark wiggle)?

6. Respond to the following question:

$$\overline{\text{PRO}^{\rightarrow X}\ \text{HUNGRY}}^{\text{Q}}$$

7. What does this sign mean?

8. What does this sign mean?

9. What does this sign mean?

10. What does this sign mean?

CHAPTER 9

Describing People and Things

In this chapter, you will learn how to describe people and things. We will begin with the vocabulary that is most often used when providing descriptions, then move on to how to create sentences using that vocabulary. You can find all of the following signs in the chapter on the DVD, along with additional vocabulary and example sentences.

Colors

Colors are a basic building block in describing people (hair color, eye color) as well as things (clothes, cars, nature). Knowing this vocabulary is useful, as colors are often used to identify things.

Color

COLOR

Red

RED

Orange

ORANGE

Yellow

YELLOW

Green

GREEN

Blue

BLUE

Purple

PURPLE

Black

BLACK

Brown

BROWN

White

WHITE

Pink

PINK

Gray

GRAY

These are the basic colors, but we all know that the world isn't composed of only these few. We may describe the sky as "light blue" and a shirt as "greenish." ASL can express these differences as well. Instead of adding a word (*light* or *dark*) or morpheme (*-ish*) as English does, ASL modifies how the sign is made and the facial expression used in producing it. To convey the idea that something is a lighter shade, you round your lips almost like you are blowing through them. You also squint your eyes slightly. The sign itself is produced a bit slower, almost gently. Here is an example:

Light blue

LIGHT-BLUE

If you want to convey the idea that something is "reddish" or "yellowish," you use the same facial expression, but instead of making the sign gently, you make it with a clipped movement and duplicate that movement. The following is an example:

Reddish

REDDISH

The intensity or laxness of your face and how you produce the sign contribute additional meaning to the varying shades or hues you are describing.

Textures, Surfaces, and Sizes

Another way of describing something is by explaining its texture (scratchy, soft), what the surface is like (smooth, bumpy), or its size (small, large). Let's learn some of the vocabulary used in these types of descriptions:

Soft   **Rough**

SOFT   **ROUGH**

Hard

HARD

Smooth

SMOOTH

Small/little

SMALL

SMALL AMOUNT

Large

LARGE

LARGE

Tall

TALL

TALL

Short

SHORT

Skinny   ### Fat

SKINNY   **FAT**

As with colors, you may need to modify the signs to match what you are describing more accurately. For instance, if you were talking about someone who plays in the NBA, you wouldn't just describe him as tall, but more likely as *very* tall. To express this in ASL, you would modify how you produced the sign TALL and add in facial expressions to intensify the description. Compare the sign for TALL and the one for VERY-TALL:

TALL   **VERY-TALL**

Here are some other examples to give you an idea of how depictive signs can be modified to more closely represent the entity being explained:

Bumpy versus very bumpy

BUMP   **VERY-BUMPY**

Large versus very large

LARGE   **VERY-LARGE**

Shapes

One of the advantages of ASL is that you can visually represent the entity you are attempting to describe. Learning to capitalize on the visual aspect of the language allows you to provide descriptions more effectively. This becomes apparent when you look at how ASL expresses shapes:

Shape   ## Square

SHAPE   **SQUARE**

Circle/round

CIRCLE

BALL

Triangle

Box

TRIANGLE

BOX

As you can see, the signs are similar to the shape of the entity they describe. The signs can also be modified to reflect the size of the object. Compare the BOX sign used to describe a small jewelry box versus the one for a large box:

Small Jewelry Box

Large Jewelry Box

BOX

BOX

In the first instance, the signer produces a tiny box by moving her hands together to make the shape. In the second, she creates a much larger box by moving her arms wide apart and extending them outward as well. The key to describing objects effectively is to visually represent what they look like with your hands and sometimes your body.

Positioning

When talking about people and things, you also need to describe them in relation to one another. In English, this is most often accomplished with the use of prepositional phrases: *on, in, under, over, next to, near,* and so on. In ASL, it is more common to demonstrate the relationship between entities by using your hands, arms, and body, as well as the space around you, to depict these relationships. ASL also uses prepositions in some instances, such as when signing ON MONDAY or KEY ON TABLE.

To illustrate how this works, let's begin with the English sentence "The cup is on the table." In English, we typically identify the entity first—in this case, "the cup"—and then where it can be found—"on the table." The preposition *on* signals the relationship between the two objects. The cup is making contact with the top surface of the table. It is, of course, possible to say "The table is under the cup," but this would sound slightly odd to most English speakers.

In ASL, it is more common to identify the location (the table) first and then what was placed there (the cup). The relationship between the entities is determined by where the hand representing the cup is placed in relation to the table. It is not necessary to produce a sign for the English preposition *on* because this information is given through the signs TABLE and CUP. This is what it would look like in ASL:

CUP ON TABLE

The signer begins by producing the sign TABLE, then she leaves the nondominant arm where it is and uses the dominant arm to make the sign CUP and place it on top of the nondominant arm. The fact that the ulnar side of her hand is in contact with her forearm informs us that the cup is "on" the table. We can see the relationship between the two entities. As you may have guessed, if you wanted to express that the cup is under the table (or that the table is over the cup), you would alter the position of the sign CUP in relation to TABLE:

This principle of visually demonstrating where entities are in relation to one another is the basis for many descriptions in ASL. Although it is fairly straightforward, it can be challenging for English speakers to give up the use of prepositions. This is not to say that ASL doesn't have lexical signs for these concepts; they are just used far less frequently than in English.

Let's learn how to describe a room. Suppose you want to describe the layout of the following bedroom:

You begin by establishing the point of reference, in this case, where the door to the room is. Then you can describe the room as if you were standing in the doorway. A description might look something like this:

DOOR ENTER

WALL

WINDOWS FLAT-ENTITY-BE-AT$^{\rightarrow L}$

WINDOW BED BED-BUOY WINDOW-BUOY

TABLE BUOY

BED TABLE

DESK LIGHT

As you can see, the signer identifies an entity and then positions it in relation to another entity.

You can use the same principles to describe a person in relation to other people. If you wanted, for example, to explain how you were standing in line at the store and a man came up and stood behind you, it would look like this:

PRO-1 STAND UPRIGHT-PERSON STAND

MAN UPRIGHT-PERSON-WALK-TOWARD

The signer uses her two extended fingers to demonstrate where she was and where the man was in relation to her. If the clerk at the store was slow and the line became longer, the signer could describe this in the following way:

MANY-UPRIGHT-PEOPLE-IN-LINE

If things got really busy, the line might have begun to wind around to allow everyone to fit. This would be expressed in the following way:

MANY-UPRIGHT-PEOPLE-IN-LINE

Putting It All Together

Now that you have learned several aspects to describing people and things, let's look at some examples of how they can be combined. I will provide an English sentence and an example of how it would be expressed in ASL:

The girl has brown hair.

GIRL THERE HAIR BROWN

ASL has a specific lexical sign that means "blond hair." It looks like this:

BLOND

He has blond hair.

PRO→ˣ BLOND

That man is tall and thin.

MAN THERE TALL THIN

The car is blue.

CAR BLUE

The room is light pink with white vertical stripes.

WALLS LIGHT-PINK WHITE STRIPES

Notice that in the last description, the direction of the white stripes is provided as well. The signer produces the sign STRIPE starting at her face and moving her hand downward. If the stripes were horizontal, she could have started to her left and moved her hand across her body like this:

WALLS LIGHT-PINK WHITE STRIPES

Chapter Summary

You now know the basics for describing people and things. When describing things in ASL, you need to remember to visually represent what you see. Take advantage of the fact that you can use your hands and body to position things in the space around you, as well as to demonstrate the size of objects.

In this chapter, you learned the following:

1. Signs for colors, including how to modify the signs to express different hues and intensities.

2. How to describe different textures, surfaces, and sizes, including some basic vocabulary. Again, the signs can be modified by changing how they are produced to reflect the appropriate size of objects.

3. The vocabulary for some basic shapes, which can also be tailored to match the object being described.

4. How to use the space around you to partially demonstrate how things are positioned in relation to one another. The use of prepositions is minimized because of your ability to use your hands to reflect this relationship.

QUIZ

All the sentences used in this quiz can be viewed on the DVD. You will need to view the sentences being signed in order to answer the questions.

1. The signer is describing her cat. What color(s) is the cat?

2. The signer is describing the paint color she chose for her baby's nursery. What color is it?

3. How is the signer describing her bed?

4. The signer is describing a person. What is she saying?

5. The signer is describing a person. What is she saying?

6. What does this sign mean?

7. How is the signer describing the shape of a paper?

8. Where did the signer find her book?

9. The signer is describing her bedroom. Where is her bed?

10. The signer is describing a woman. What color hair does the woman have?

CHAPTER 10

Expressing Likes and Dislikes

In this chapter, you will learn a lot of vocabulary that you can use to express what you like and don't like. This will include signs to explain the reasons for those likes and dislikes. Next, you will learn some basic sentences using the vocabulary. You can find all of the following signs in this chapter on the DVD, along with additional vocabulary and example sentences.

Preferences

This section presents signs that are used to express preferences:

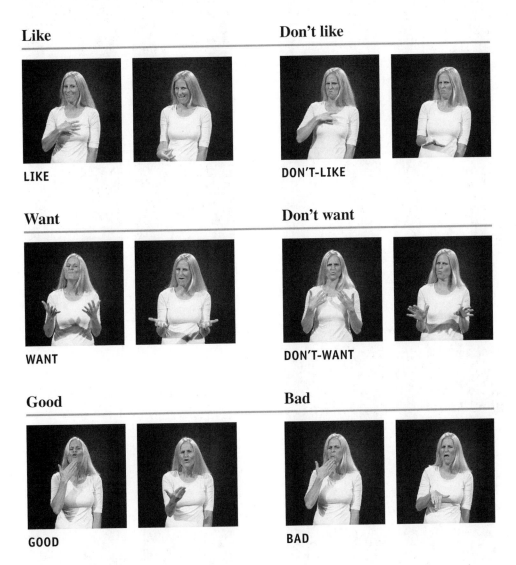

Like

LIKE

Don't like

DON'T-LIKE

Want

WANT

Don't want

DON'T-WANT

Good

GOOD

Bad

BAD

Notice that the hands are turned downward whenever a sign expresses a negative.

Enjoy

ENJOY

Delicious

DELICIOUS

Love

LOVE

Adore

KISS-FIST

Same

SAME

Better

BETTER

Best

BEST

Notice that the difference between BETTER and BEST is the final location of the hand. When producing BETTER, the hand is at the midface, but with BEST, it is near the forehead.

Satisfied

SATISFIED

Champ

CHAMP

The sign CHAMP is used when describing people or things that are the best at what they do or are the top in a specific field. It provides a strong endorsement for the entity. It would similar to saying "These are the most delicious muffins" in English.

Worst

WORST

Disgust

DISGUST

Equal

EQUAL

Awful

AWFUL

Awful (female)

AWFUL

Nice

NICE

Typically, the sign for AWFUL is used only by women. It conveys a sense of sympathy, as in "Oh, that's awful. I'm sorry that happened."

Cool/Neat

COOL

Cool

COOL

Doesn't matter

DOESN'T MATTER

Maybe

MAYBE

Lousy

LOUSY

Fun

FUN

This response also incorporates the feeling that you are impressed by the creativity or uniqueness of something.

Thrilled

THRILLED

Excited

EXCITED

Evaluative Signs

Depressed

DEPRESSED

Boring

BORING

Beautiful

BEAUTIFUL

Ugly

UGLY

Delicious

DELICIOUS

Dirty

DIRTY

Clean

CLEAN

More

MORE

Need

NEED

Right/correct

RIGHT

Wrong

WRONG

Additional Concepts

Strange/odd/weird

STRANGE

Important

IMPORTANT

Win

WIN

Cancel

CANCEL

Cancel

CANCEL CANCEL CANCEL CANCEL

This is an indicating verb that can be directed in space. If you were talking with someone about different meetings or obligations you needed to cancel, you could direct the sign toward the areas with token spaces that you have established to represent the different activities.

Wow

WOW

Wow/whoa

WHOA

Trouble

TROUBLE

Wonderful

WONDERFUL

Warn

WARN

This is an indicating verb, which means how it is produced gives information about the subject and object. If you are warning someone else who is present, you would direct the sign toward that person. If you want to convey that someone is warning you, you would produce the sign near your body with the fingertips of the active hand facing you.

Expressing Yourself

Now you will learn some ways to use these signs. The English sentence is listed first, followed by how it is signed in ASL.

I like him.

PRO-1 LIKE PRO$^{\rightarrow X}$

He likes cats.

PRO$^{\rightarrow X}$ LIKE CAT

She doesn't like dogs.

PRO$^{\rightarrow X}$ DON'T-LIKE DOG

Do you like the color blue?

PRO→ˣ LIKE COLOR BLUE

I enjoy reading.

PRO-1 ENJOY READ

Notice that in ASL the sign ENJOY is used to express pleasure or enjoyment of something.

Which do you prefer, red or white wine?

PRO→ˣ PREFER RED WINE WHITE WINE, WHICH

She doesn't want to go to school.

PRO→ˣ DOESN'T-WANT GO SCHOOL

I love my daughter.

PRO-1 LOVE POSS-1 DAUGHTER

The food is delicious.

FOOD DELICIOUS

My car is dirty.

POSS-1 CAR DIRTY

I need to clean my car.

PRO-1 NEED CLEAN POSS-1 CAR

I want to learn more ASL.

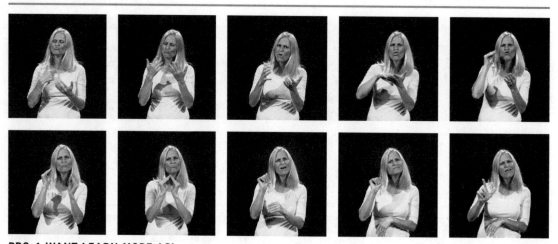

PRO-1 WANT LEARN MORE ASL

He is strange.

PRO→X STRANGE

Wow! I can't believe I won!

WOW PRO-1 CAN'T BELIEVE PRO-1 WIN

Notice how the signer uses facial expressions when producing these sentences. As we discussed in Chapter 9, you can vary the intensity of something by changing your facial expression.

Chapter Summary

In this chapter, you learned the following:

1. The vocabulary for expressing your likes and dislikes.
2. The vocabulary for evaluating objects.
3. Additional vocabulary to express preferences.
4. How to use this vocabulary to express your preferences and reactions.

QUIZ

All the sentences used in this quiz can be viewed on the DVD. You will need to view the sentences being signed in order to answer the questions.

1. Does the signer like or dislike the color red?
2. Does the signer want coffee?
3. How is the signer describing the meal she ate?
4. The signer is critiquing a movie she recently saw. What did she think?
5. How is the signer describing her car?
6. Does the signer want more food?
7. Did the signer's team win or lose?
8. How is the signer describing a man she just met?
9. What is the signer asking?
10. Does the signer want to go home?

CHAPTER 11

Expressing Past, Present, and Future

Up until now, almost all the sentences you have been learning have been in the present tense. You are probably itching to talk about topics that happened to you yesterday, last week, or when you were in high school. You are also probably wondering how to discuss future events.

In this chapter, you will learn how ASL expresses tenses. As you read in Chapter 1, English and ASL are independent languages and therefore have different structures for expressing the same concepts and information. The description of past, present, and future is one area in which the languages differ significantly. It is worth remembering that the goal when learning a new language is to learn how to express the same concepts, not the same structures. Remind yourself of this as you work through this chapter.

Expressing Things That Happened in the Past

The most significant difference between the ASL and English tense systems is the fact that ASL does not mark verbs for tense. In English, for example, if you read or hear the sentence "I walked home," you know the action has already occurred. The event is in the speaker's past. The morpheme -ed signals when the event occurred. When indicating the past tense in ASL, you do not add a morpheme to the verb. Instead, you use a sign indicating that something has been completed or identifying a specific time in the past, then you sign the sentence as you would for the present tense.

Let's first look at the lexical signs used to mark a sentence as having occurred in the past.

FINISH

The sign FINISH used in this context means that the action/event has been completed. You can produce it at the beginning or the end of the sentence to signal when the action happened.

YESTERDAY

The sign YESTERDAY means the day before today. You produce this sign at the beginning or the end of the sentence.

TWO-DAYS-AGO

The sign TWO-DAYS-AGO means two days prior to today. You can produce it at the beginning or the end of the sentence.

LAST-WEEK

The sign LAST-WEEK means the week prior to the current one. You can produce it at the beginning or the end of the sentence.

LAST-MONTH

The sign LAST-MONTH means the month prior to the current one. You can produce it at the beginning or the end of the sentence.

LAST-YEAR

The sign LAST-YEAR means the year prior to the current one. You can produce it at the beginning or the end of the sentence.

LONG-AGO

The sign LONG-AGO indicates a time period in the distant past, such as when an adult talks about his childhood. You can change how you produce the sign to indicate a time even further back. It would look like this:

LONG-LONG-AGO

Notice that the signer's facial expression changes, and the size of the sign itself is bigger.

To produce sentences in the past tense, you use one of these signs to mark the action/event as having occurred in the past. Let's look at some examples. I will list the English sentence first, followed by how it is produced in ASL. (These and more examples are on the DVD.)

I ate.

PRO-1 FINISH EAT

She read the book.

PRO→ˣ FINISH READ BOOK

He walked home yesterday.

YESTERDAY PRO→ˣ WALK HOME

He left last week.

PRO→ˣ LEAVE LAST-WEEK

When I was a kid, I played soccer.

LONG-AGO PRO-1 YOUNG PRO-1 PLAY SOCCER

Once you have marked that you are speaking in the past tense, it is assumed that this continues until you indicate a change to the present or future. For example, if you began with the sentence LONG-AGO PRO-1 YOUNG PRO-1 PLAY SOCCER and then continued with PRO-1 PRACTICE EVERYDAY, the latter would mean "I practiced every day." The tense would be understood to be the past because it continues the sequence of events that happened "LONG-AGO."

Expressing Things That Are Happening in the Present

Present tense is the default setting in ASL. Unless you indicate otherwise, it is assumed that what you are signing is in the present tense. The examples given in earlier chapters were all in the present tense. If you change to another tense and

want to return to present tense, you can use the following lexical signs to indicate that you are referring to the present:

Now (present)　　　　　　　　　　**Today (present day)**

NOW　　　　　　　　　　　　　　　TODAY

Expressing Things That Will Happen

The future tense in ASL is similar to the future tense in English in that a lexical sign identifies that the action or event is forthcoming. In English the word *will* is used to indicate something is to occur in the future; for instance, "I will go home." ASL has several lexical signs that are used to mark a sentence as future tense.

Will (future time)

WILL

You can increase the time between the present and the time of the upcoming event by increasing the distance you extend your hand in front of your body.

Far into the future

The sign FUTURE does not guarantee that the event will occur, but rather conveys the possibility that it will. The sign WILL, however, implies certainty that the event will transpire.

Tomorrow

The sign TOMORROW means the day after today. It is signed at the beginning or the end of a sentence to signal when an event will happen.

Next week

The sign NEXT-WEEK means the week following the current one. It is signed at the beginning or the end of the sentence.

Next month

    The sign NEXT-MONTH means the month following the current one. It is signed at the beginning or the end of the sentence.

Next year

    The sign NEXT-YEAR means the year following the current one. It is signed at the beginning or the end of the sentence.

    To produce sentences in the future tense, you use one of these signs to mark the sentence appropriately. Let's look at some examples. I will list the English sentence first, followed by how it is produced in ASL.

I will eat later.

PRO-1 WILL EAT LATER

I'll run a marathon someday.

PRO-1 FUTURE RUN #MARATHON

My appointment is tomorrow.

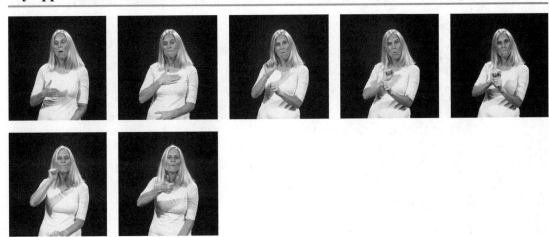

POSS-1 APPOINTMENT TOMORROW

Classes begin next week.

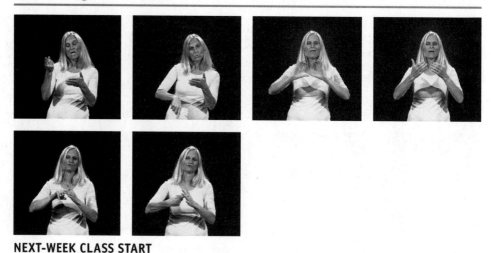

NEXT-WEEK CLASS START

She starts college next year.

NEXT-YEAR PRO→ˣ START COLLEGE

As with the other tenses, once you have established that you are referring to a future time, this understanding remains until you indicate that you are referring to a different time.

Let's look at a couple of examples in which the signer changes tenses. The English sentences are provided first, followed by how they are expressed in ASL.

Last week I worked. This week I am on vacation.

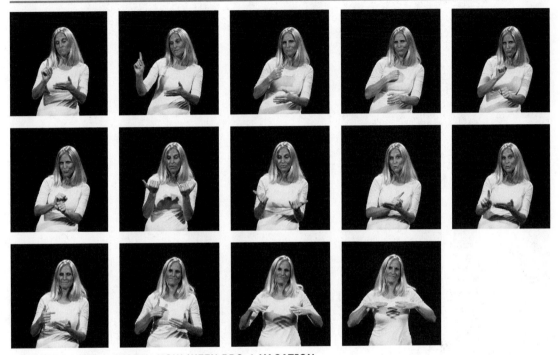

LAST-WEEK PRO-1 WORK. NOW WEEK PRO-1 VACATION.

American Sign Language Demystified

I am reading the book. When I finish, I will give it to you.

PRO-1 READ BOOK. PRO-1 FINISH, WILL GIVE.

Last year I visited Italy. Next year I will visit France.

LAST-YEAR PRO-1 VISIT ITALY. NEXT-YEAR PRO-1 VISIT FRANCE.

Spatial Timeline

ASL uses space to establish when things happen. As you have seen, signs that refer to things that happened in the past end behind the signer, signs about the present are produced directly in front of the signer, and those that refer to things that will happen end in front of the signer. Events in time are mapped onto a spatial timeline of sorts, as illustrated in the following diagram:

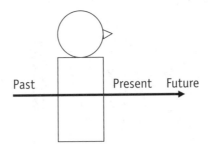

Signers can indicate how far in the past events have occurred—or how far in the future they will occur—by using this visual timeline.

Chapter Summary

In this chapter, you learned the following:

1. How to express actions or events that occurred in the past.
2. How to express actions or events that are occurring in the present.
3. How to express actions or events that will occur in the future.
4. How to change between past, present, and future tenses.
5. How to use a spatial timeline to indicate when actions and events have happened or will happen.

QUIZ

All the sentences used in this quiz can be viewed on the DVD. You will need to view the sentences being signed in order to answer the questions.

1. Is this sentence expressing something from the past, present, or future?
2. Is this sentence expressing something from the past, present, or future?
3. Is this sentence expressing something from the past, present, or future?
4. Is this sentence expressing something from the past, present, or future?
5. When did the signer leave?
6. When is the signer's appointment?
7. When will the signer practice?
8. When was the signer reading?
9. When did the signer leave?
10. When was the signer on vacation?

CHAPTER 12

The Manual Alphabet: Finger Spelling

The ASL manual alphabet represents the Roman orthographic system. While these two systems are related, not all signs in the ASL manual alphabet resemble the English letter they represent, as you will see in a minute. Each letter is considered to be an individual sign. Finger spelling is used for proper names of people, places (cities and some states), titles (books, movies), and brand names, as well as to clarify the meaning of a sign (this often happens when people are unfamiliar with a particular regional sign). Finger spelling can also be used to emphasize a particular word and draw additional attention to it during discourse. You are likely to finger spell English words for which you don't know the equivalent ASL sign. Finger spelling is actually used in three ways: one is referred to as *careful finger spelling*; the second is with *lexicalized signs*; and the third is *rapid finger spelling*.

You use one hand to produce the ASL manual alphabet. Not all sign languages follow this convention. The British manual alphabet, for example, requires the use of two hands. You will want to use your dominant hand to finger spell. You should bend

your arm at the elbow and position your hand near your shoulder at chest level. Your palm should face out, toward the person to whom you are signing (you should see the back of your hand). This makes it easier for the other person to see the letters.

The ASL Manual Alphabet

Let's see what the manual alphabet looks like (refer also to the DVD):

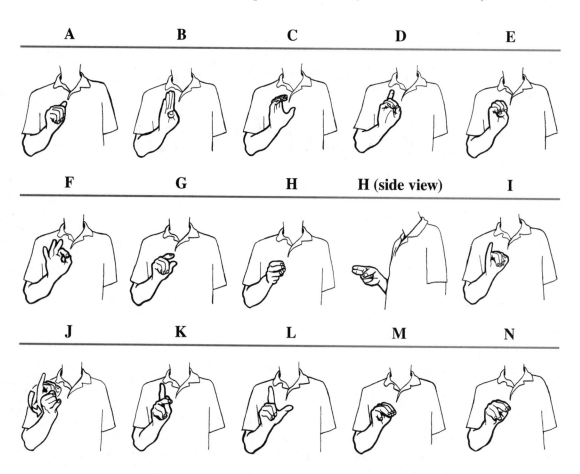

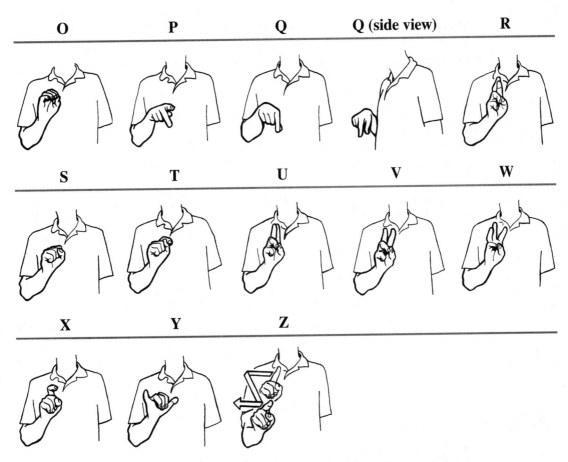

As you can see, some finger spelled signs look like the written English letter they represent, such as *C, L, O,* and *V.* Others, such as *G, R, S,* and *X,* look different.

Careful Finger Spelling

Careful finger spelling refers to finger spelling in which each letter of an English word is produced. For example, you use this when telling someone your name for the first time. The intention is for the other person to be able to see and identify all the letters in the word to help ensure comprehension. When the same word is finger spelled several times in the course of a conversation, the letters are held for a shorter

time each time, and some may even be omitted after a while. This is especially true with words that have many letters. As a finger spelled word becomes more condensed, you always retain the first and last letters of the word. Generally speaking, it is better to maintain clarity and sacrifice speed when finger spelling.

There are some conventions used in finger spelling. You want to produce clear signs, and the transitions between the letters should be smooth. Do not bounce your hand up and down or forward and back when finger spelling; keep it as stationary as possible. When finger spelling more than one word at a time—for instance, your first and last name—insert a short pause between the words. For instance, when spelling "Jane Smith," you would pause after J-A-N-E. (See the DVD.)

If a word has two of the same letters in a row, you drag your hand slightly to the side to indicate that the letter is repeated. For instance, the two *l*'s in "William."

More often than not, producing finger spelling is easier to learn than understanding it. A tip for comprehension is not to worry about identifying each individual letter, but to look at the signs as a whole. It is similar to reading a word. If you see the word *cat*, you don't say to yourself, "*C-a-t*," and identify the individual letters; you perceive the entire word. Say you are having a conversation with someone about fruit and he signs a word. You only identify the letters W-A-T-R-M-E-L-N, but you can fill in the missing letters yourself to make *watermelon*. The context can often provide clues as to what is being finger spelled.

Lexicalized Signs

The second way the ASL manual alphabet is used is in lexicalized signs, which occur when finger spelled words become their own sign. The individual letters are changed in such a way that they no longer look like their careful finger spelling counterparts. Look at the DVD, and compare two representations of the English word *job* using careful finger spelling and a lexicalized sign.

In careful finger spelling, you see three distinct letters, J-O-B. The palm of the hand is directed outward for the production of each letter. This contrasts with the lexicalized version #JOB. The J is produced the same in both versions, the O is omitted, and the B is produced with the palm facing the signer in the lexicalized version.

Frequently used words become lexicalized over time and sometimes hardly resemble their original form. Here is a list of commonly used lexicalized signs:

Yes

#YES

The sign #YES is a positive response to a question, often used as an emphatic response.

OK

#OK

The sign #OK is a positive response to a question or used to tell someone that you are following what is being said. It can be directed in space, so you can direct it toward a person or entity if you want to distinguish the answer you are giving that person from others.

No

#NO

The sign #NO is a negative response to a question and carries a more serious or emphatic tone.

Wow

#WOW

The sign #WOW is used to indicate that you are impressed by something unexpected. This sign is produced simultaneously on both hands.

What

#WHAT

The sign #WHAT is used to indicate surprise about information that has just been received. This sign can also be produced simultaneously on both hands for added emphasis.

Early

#EARLY

E-mail

E#MAIL

The sign can be used as an indicating verb and be directed toward the person to whom you want to send an electronic message.

Too bad

#TB

The sign is used as a response to someone who may be upset about a decision or situation.

Bank

#BANK

Apartment

#APT

Television

#TV

All

#ALL

The sign #ALL means everyone or everything. It can be directed in space to identify the entities involved.

Suppose

#IF

No good

#NG

The sign #NG is used as an evaluative comment on a situation.

Ha ha

#HA #HA

The sign #HA means that a person thinks something is funny and is amused by it. The sign is typically repeated. If the sign is produced only once, it is often a sarcastic response to something far-fetched.

Oh

#OH

The sign #OH is an exclamation similar to the English "oh."

#DO-#DO

The sign #DO-DO translates as "doing something." It is most often produced on both hands at the same time. If it is accompanied by a WH- question nonmanual signal, it means "What are you doing?"

#AC

The sign #AC means "air-conditioning."

#HS

The sign #HS means "high school."

#UPSET

The sign #UPSET means "to be upset about something."

#DA

The sign #DA means "disabled."

Chapter Summary

In this chapter, you learned the following:

1. That finger spelling is used for proper names, titles, and brand names; to clarify the meaning of a sign; and to request the sign for an English concept.

2. The twenty-six signs for the ASL manual alphabet.

3. How to produce finger spelling by using your dominant hand, producing the sign near your shoulder at chest level, keeping your hand steady, and producing double letters by sliding your hand slightly to the side.

4. The definition of careful finger spelling (when each letter is deliberately produced, allowing the person watching to see each letter).

5. That lexicalized signs are those derived from finger spelling. The form often no longer resembles the original carefully finger spelled word.

6. Common lexicalized signs and their meanings.

QUIZ

All the sentences used in this quiz can be viewed on the DVD. You will need to view the sentences being signed in order to answer the questions.

1. Did the signer produce careful finger spelling or a lexicalized sign?
2. Did the signer produce careful finger spelling or a lexicalized sign?
3. Did the signer produce careful finger spelling or a lexicalized sign?
4. Did the signer produce careful finger spelling or a lexicalized sign?
5. Did the signer produce careful finger spelling or a lexicalized sign?
6. What word did the signer spell?
7. What word did the signer spell?
8. Where did the signer say she went?
9. Where does the signer live?
10. What does the signer like?

CHAPTER 13

Numbers, Dates, and Time

In this chapter, you will learn ASL numbers and how to use them to communicate things like dates and time. Numbers are similar to finger spelling in that they are made using your dominant hand. You can also recombine them with other morphemes to produce more complex forms.

ASL Numbers

Let's first learn the basic number system in ASL. Numbers one through five can be produced with the palm facing either toward or away from the signer. When counting in normal conversational situations, they are produced with the palm facing the signer. You can turn the palm away from you if you are signing from a distance and want to make sure the number can be seen or if you are emphasizing the number for some reason. Starting with six, the palm faces outward toward the person to whom you are signing.

Numbers

NUMBERS

0	1	2	3	4	5

ZERO	ONE	TWO	THREE	FOUR	FIVE

6	7	8	9	10

SIX	SEVEN	EIGHT	NINE	TEN

11		12	

ELEVEN   **TWELVE**

13

THIRTEEN

14

FOURTEEN

15

FIFTEEN

For the numbers sixteen through nineteen, there are two ways to articulate the signs. Each is presented here.

16

SIXTEEN   **SIXTEEN**

17

SEVENTEEN   SEVENTEEN

18

EIGHTEEN   EIGHTEEN

19

NINETEEN   NINETEEN

20   **21**

TWENTY   TWENTY-ONE

22

TWENTY-TWO

23

TWENTY-THREE

24

TWENTY-FOUR

25

TWENTY-FIVE

26

TWENTY-SIX

27

TWENTY-SEVEN

28

TWENTY-EIGHT

29

TWENTY-NINE

30

THIRTY

Things are simpler from here on. For the numbers thirty-one through thirty-nine, forty-one through forty-nine, and so forth until ninety-nine, you combine the two numbers that are used. Here are some examples:

31

THIRTY-ONE

32

THIRTY-TWO

33

THIRTY-THREE

40

FORTY

50

FIFTY

60

SIXTY

70

SEVENTY

80

EIGHTY

90

NINETY

100

ONE HUNDRED

200

TWO HUNDRED

300

THREE HUNDRED

400

500

FOUR HUNDRED

FIVE HUNDRED

600

700

SIX HUNDRED

SEVEN HUNDRED

800

900

EIGHT HUNDRED

NINE HUNDRED

To count in the hundreds you combine the signs for HUNDRED plus the additional number. For numbers higher than one hundred, you combine the first number, the sign HUNDRED, and the additional number. Here are some examples:

305

THREE HUNDRED FIVE

618

SIX HUNDRED EIGHTEEN

1,000   ## 2,000

ONE THOUSAND   **TWO THOUSAND**

For numbers higher than one thousand, you combine the first number, the sign THOUSAND, and the additional number. A number such as 6,452 would look like this:

SIX THOUSAND FOUR HUNDRED FIFTY TWO

If you want to express a fraction, you sign the numerator first, then move the sign downward to express the denominator:

½   ⅝

ONE over TWO   **FIVE over EIGHT**

Ordinal Numbers

If you want to place things in order, you need to use the following ASL signs for ordinal numbers. Each is produced with a slight twist of the wrist.

First   **Second**

FIRST   **SECOND**

Third

THIRD

Fourth

FOURTH

Fifth

FIFTH

If you want to express the order of entrants finished in a competition, you produce the signs differently. Rather than twist only, you twist and move the hand so it becomes horizontal.

First place

FIRST PLACE

Second place

SECOND PLACE

Third place

THIRD PLACE

Age

In Chapter 3, you learned about the prefix $\{AGE_0\}$, which means "age of living thing." It is made by having a finger make contact with the chin. When combined with a number, it means "years old." Here are some examples:

One year old

$\{AGE_0\}$ONE

Five years old

$\{AGE_0\}$FIVE

Fifteen years old

$\{AGE_0\}$FIFTEEN

Thirty years old

$\{AGE_0\}$THIRTY

Fifty-five years old

{AGE$_0$}FIFTY-FIVE

To indicate approximate age, such as "in his or her fifties," you use the morpheme {APPROXIMATE-DECADE}, which is produced by directing the palm to the side and shaking the hand slightly. Look at this example:

{AGE$_0$}{APPROXIMATE-DECADE}FIVE

Money

This section looks at how ASL numbers are used to express prices.
   First is the sign that means "dollar":

DOLLAR

To express a dollar amount from one to nine, you show the number with the palm facing outward, then quickly twist the sign so the palm is facing you. It looks like this:

FIVE DOLLAR

For amounts of ten dollars and more, you specify a dollar amount by first producing the number sign followed by the sign DOLLAR:

Ten dollars

TEN DOLLAR

The sign that means "cents/penny" is as follows:

CENTS

This sign combines with number signs to create the following:

Nickel

NICKEL

Dime

DIME

Quarter

QUARTER

Dates

Let's begin by learning some vocabulary to talk about dates. Some of these will be familiar from Chapter 11.

Calendar

CALENDAR

Day

DAY

Today

TODAY

Yesterday

YESTERDAY

Tomorrow

TOMORROW

Week

WEEK

Last week

LAST-WEEK

Next week

NEXT-WEEK

Month

MONTH

Next month

NEXT-MONTH

Year

YEAR

Next year

NEXT-YEAR

Last year

LAST-YEAR

You can combine numbers with the signs for DAY, WEEK, MONTH, and YEAR. Anytime a number is combined with a sign, it is referred to as *numerical incorporation*. Here are some examples:

Three days

THREE-DAY

Four weeks

FOUR-WEEK

Five months

FIVE-MONTH

Here are the signs for the days of the week:

Monday

MONDAY

Tuesday

TUESDAY

Wednesday

WEDNESDAY

Thursday

THURSDAY

Friday

FRIDAY

Saturday

SATURDAY

Sunday

SUNDAY

The production of these signs can be altered to mean "weekly" or "biweekly," as you see here:

Every Monday   **Every other Monday**

MONDAY weekly   **MONDAY biweekly**

The signer moves the sign M downward to indicate an event is happening every Monday. If it is scheduled for every other Monday, she bounces down, "skipping" the middle Monday.

Suppose you are planning an event and want to figure out what week during the next month people are available. You can use a sideways 4, which visually represents the four weeks of the calendar month. Each finger represents a different week: the pointer is week one; the middle finger is week two; the ring finger is week three; and the pinkie is week four. By pointing with your dominant hand, you indicate the week. For instance, the third week of the month looks like this:

THIRD-WEEK-OF-MONTH

The months of the year are finger spelled, the longer months with only the first few letters (see the DVD for all the months):

January

J-A-N

February

F-E-B

March

M-A-R-C-H

You can combine all this vocabulary to give someone a specific date such as the following:

Monday, January 11, 1970

MONDAY J-A-N ELEVEN NINETEEN SEVENTY

Time

Numbers also figure into the expression of time. Let's first learn some basic vocabulary:

Time

TIME

Second (unit of time)

 #SEC

Minute

 MINUTE

Half hour

HALF-HOUR

Hour

HOUR

Morning

MORNING

Noon

NOON

Afternoon

AFTERNOON

Evening/night

NIGHT

Midnight

MIDNIGHT

All night

ALL-NIGHT

You can use numerical incorporation to identify a specific number of minutes or hours:

Five minutes

FIVE-MINUTE

Seven hours

SEVEN-HOUR

You can incorporate numbers one through nine.

When you want to express the concept "o'clock" by combining the sign TIME with a number, it looks like this:

One o'clock

ONE O'CLOCK

Five o'clock

FIVE O'CLOCK

If you want to express a specific time, you first sign TIME and then the numbers, starting with the hour and followed by the minutes. To indicate A.M. or P.M., simply sign MORNING or NIGHT:

2:45 A.M.

TIME TWO FORTY FIVE MORNING

It is also possible to express the concept of "every" with some of these signs. If something occurs daily at noon, for example, you use this sign:

NOON daily

Every night

NIGHT daily

Chapter Summary

In this chapter, you learned the following:

1. How to sign numbers from 1 to 999,999.
2. How to express fractions.
3. How to express ordinal numbers.
4. How to express placement, as in a competition.
5. How to express age.
6. The vocabulary used to discuss money and how to express costs.
7. How to express dates, including the vocabulary for the days of the week and the months.
8. How to express time.

QUIZ

All the sentences used in this quiz can be viewed on the DVD. You will need to view the sentences being signed in order to answer the questions.

1. What is the signer's apartment number?
2. How many cats does the signer's mom have?
3. How many books did the signer borrow from the library?
4. How many people attended the soccer game?

5. In what place did the signer's team finish in the tournament?
6. How old is the signer's father?
7. When does the signer have class?
8. When does the signer wake up?
9. What month does school start?
10. How much money did the signer lose?

CHAPTER 14

Family and Friends

In this chapter, you will learn vocabulary to use in discussing friends and family. This includes words and phrases for talking about activities in which you participate. The text tells you what you will find on the DVD and offers explanations of some signs. All the glosses are included, and many are the same as the English terms.

Family

We will begin with the vocabulary used to express concepts related to the family. You will notice that signs referring to females are articulated on the lower part of the face (the cheek and chin) and signs referring to males are articulated higher on the face (the forehead and temple).

Family

FAMILY

Mother

MOTHER

Father

FATHER

Brother

BROTHER

Sister

SISTER

Child

CHILD

Children

CHILDREN

Adult

ADULT

Step-

STEP-

Aunt

AUNT

Uncle

UNCLE

Son

SON

Daughter

DAUGHTER

Grandmother

GRANDMOTHER

Grandfather

GRANDFATHER

Nephew

NEPHEW

Niece

NIECE

Cousin

COUSIN (female)

COUSIN (male)

Unlike English, ASL has gender-specific signs for female and male cousins. The sign for a female cousin is made on the lower half of the face, and the sign for a male cousin is made near the forehead.

Wedding

WEDDING

Bride

#BRIDE

Groom

#GROOM

Marry   ## Husband

MARRY   HUSBAND

Wife   ## Partner

WIFE   PARTNER

Divorce

In-law

DIVORCE

IN-LAW

The IN-LAW sign is used together with the sign for the relative you want to label as an in-law, such as the following:

Sister-in-law

SISTER-IN-LAW

Mother-in-law

MOTHER-IN-LAW

Pregnant

PREGNANT

Born

BIRTH

Baby

BABY

Miscarry

MISCARRY

Adopt

ADOPT

Die

DIE

Funeral

FUNERAL

House

HOUSE

Home

HOME

Kiss

KISS

Hug

HUG

Friends

Friend

FRIEND

Best friend

BEST-FRIEND

Boy

BOY

Girl

GIRL

Man

MAN

Woman

WOMAN

Person

PERSON

People

PEOPLE

Meet

MEET

This is an indicating verb, so it can be directed in space to indicate who is meeting whom.

Introduce

INTRODUCE

This is an indicating verb, so it can be directed in space to indicate who is being introduced to whom.

Date (verb)   ### Fall in love

DATE   **FALL-IN**

Like

LIKE

Love

LOVE

Gay

#GAY

Lesbian

LESBIAN

Straight

STRAIGHT

Flirt

FLIRT

Flatter

FLATTER

Desire

HUNGER

Gossip

GOSSIP

Chat (two variations)

CHAT

CHAT

Socialize

SOCIALIZE

Single

SINGLE

Events Shared with Family and Friends

Holiday

HOLIDAY

Valentine's Day

HEART DAY

Easter   Passover

EASTER   **PASSOVER**

Halloween (three variations)

HALLOWEEN (Vs by eyes)

HALLOWEEN (B cover eyes and remove)

HALLOWEEN (14 fingers down face)

Thanksgiving

THANKSGIVING

Christmas

CHRISTMAS

Hanukkah

HANUKKAH

Birthday (two variations)

BIRTHDAY (3 finger chin chest)

BIRTHDAY (pull on earlobe)

Anniversary   Vacation

ANNIVERSARY

VACATION

Sports (two variations)

SPORTS

#SPORTS

Basketball

BASKETBALL

Baseball

BASEBALL

Football

FOOTBALL

Volleyball

VOLLEYBALL

Swimming

SWIMMING

Hockey

HOCKEY

Skating

SKATING

Skiing

SKIING

Snowboarding

SNOWBOARDING

Skateboarding

SKATEBOARDING

Soccer

SOCCER

Running

RUN

Tennis

TENNIS

Wrestling

WRESTLING

Chapter Summary

This chapter focused on friends and family. You learned the following:

1. Vocabulary for talking about your family.
2. Vocabulary for talking about your friends.
3. Vocabulary for events shared with friends and family.

QUIZ

All the sentences used in this quiz can be viewed on the DVD. You will need to view the sentences being signed in order to answer the questions.

1. How many siblings does the signer's mom have?
2. How many children does the signer have?
3. Whose wedding did the signer attend?
4. The signer is describing a person. What did she say?
5. In what sports does the signer participate?
6. How long has the signer been snowboarding?
7. Is the signer married, single, or divorced?
8. How many people are in the signer's family?
9. What did the girl do?
10. What holiday is the signer celebrating?

CHAPTER 15

Health

In this chapter, you will learn vocabulary for discussing your health and health-related issues. The body is incorporated into many of the signs because you can point to the area you are discussing. The text tells you what you will find on the DVD and offers explanations for some of the relevant signs. All the glosses are included, and many are the same as the English terms.

Medical Professionals and Locations

Let's begin by learning the signs for medical professionals and where they work.

Doctor

DOCTOR

Nurse

NURSE

Specialist

SPECIALIST

This sign is used with others to identify a specific specialty. For example, a cardiologist would be made up of HEART and SPECIALIST; an orthopedic surgeon would be BONE and SPECIALIST.

Surgeon

SURGEON

Dentist

DENTIST

Psychiatrist

PSYCHIATRIST

Hospital

HOSPITAL

Emergency room

#ER

EMERGENCY ROOM

Operating room

SURGERY ROOM

Intensive care unit

#ICU

Ambulance

AMBULANCE

Describing Physical Ailments

This section shows how to describe how you feel or what you are experiencing physically. As you will see, you can modify the movement or location of many signs to add additional meaning. Facial expressions are also important when describing how you feel. There should be a similarity between the facial expression and the symptom. If you have a wide smile while producing the sign SICK, it will be confusing to the person with whom you are conversing.

Health

HEALTH

Help

HELP

Explain

EXPLAIN

Sick/ill

SICK

The sign you use to express the state of being sick is PRO-1 SICK. If you wanted to indicate that you have been getting sick intermittently (perhaps a symptom returns every few days), you would sign the following:

SICK intermittent

If you want to express that you have been suffering for a while, the sign is as follows:

SICK FOR MONTHS ongoing

Hurt/pain

HURT

This sign is used to express a state of being, such as in "I have pain" or "I got hurt." The sign can be moved to different locations to identify the site of the pain, as

shown by the following signs. You can also change the facial expression and the movement of the sign to demonstrate the intensity of the pain:

HURT seriously

Stomachache

Ear ache

STOMACH HURT (at stomach)

EAR HURT (at ear)

Headache

What's wrong?

HURT (at head)

WRONG

The WH- question nonmanual signal is produced simultaneously with the sign for WRONG to create the question.

Feel

FEEL

Dizzy

DIZZY

Worry

WORRY

Head cold

HEAD COLD (tissue)

Nausea

NAUSEA

Temperature

TEMPERATURE

Sore throat

SORE THROAT

Problem

PROBLEM

Breathing

BREATHING

Bruise

BLUE SPOT

#BRUISE

The sign SPOT can be moved to the location on the body where you are injured.

Cough

COUGH

Broken

BROKEN

Bone

BONE

Fracture

BONE CRACK

Torn ligament

TORN LIGAMENT

Cold (temperature)

COLD

Hot

HOT

Complain

Depressed

COMPLAIN

DEPRESSED

Weight

WEIGHT

Lose/gain weight

LOSE-WEIGHT

GAIN-WEIGHT

The first sign demonstrated means to lose weight; it looks as if weight is being removed. The second sign means to gain weight. Again, the movement can be altered to add meaning. If you wanted to express that a person had gained a large amount of weight it would look like this:

GAIN-WEIGHT a lot

Fine

FINE

Good

GOOD

So-so

SO-SO

Bad

BAD

Tired

TIRED

Vomit

VOMIT

Improve

IMPROVE

Medical Terminology

In this section you will learn vocabulary used by medical professionals.

Patient   **Surgery**

PATIENT   SURGERY

The location of this sign provides information about where the surgery happened. If you were talking about heart surgery, the sign would be moved to the chest like this:

HEART SURGERY

Medicine

MEDICINE

Pill/to take a pill

PILL

Medical history

MEDICINE HISTORY

Blood

BLOOD

Test

TEST

Blood pressure

BLOOD PRESSURE

Infection

INFECTION

Suture

SEW

Cardiopulmonary resuscitation (CPR)

#CPR

Medical resonance imaging (MRI)

#MRI

IV

#IV

Prescription

#RX

Wheelchair

WHEELCHAIR

Crutches

CRUTCHES

Cast

C-A-S-T

X-ray

X-R-A-Y

Allergy

OPPOSITE

Bandage

BANDAGE

Appointment

APPOINTMENT

Body Parts

Identifying body parts is simple. For most, you can point to the part or finger spell. This is true for the following: Ear, Eye, Mouth, Nose, Throat, Teeth, Elbow, Hip, Knuckle, Neck, Wrist, Stomach, Knee, Leg, Arm.

Some body parts have specific lexical signs:

Head

HEAD

Jaw

#JAW

Heart

HEART

Ankle

A-N-K-L-E

Chest

C-H-E-S-T

Foot/feet

F-O-O-T

F-E-E-T

Hand

HAND

Torso

T-O-R-S-O

Body

BODY

Additional Vocabulary

Bowel movement

#BM

POOP

Brush teeth

BRUSH-TEETH

Careful

CAREFUL

Drunk

DRUNK

Emotion

EMOTION

Positive

POSITIVE

Negative

NEGATIVE

Exercise

EXERCISE

Habit

HABIT

Lazy

LAZY

Need

NEED

Must

MUST

Bathroom

TOILET

Sympathy

FEEL-SORRY

Vegetarian

VEGETARIAN

Bath

BATH

Shower

SHOWER

Rest

REST

911

9-1-1

Putting It All Together

Here are several examples of how health-related vocabulary is used. The English sentence will be listed first, followed by how it is expressed in ASL.

I am sick.

PRO-1 SICK

When is your doctor appointment?

POSS⁻ˣ DOCTOR APPOINTMENT WHEN

She has gained weight.

PRO⁻ˣ GAIN-WEIGHT

He is going to have shoulder surgery.

PRO⁻ˣ WILL SURGERY at shoulder

I feel bad.

PRO-1 FEEL BAD

You must take your medicine.

PRO⁻ˣ MUST TAKE-PILL TAKE-PILL TAKE-PILL

Where is the bathroom?

wh
WHERE TOILET

The x-ray showed he broke his arm.

X-RAY SHOW ARM BROKE

Get in the habit of brushing your teeth.

PRO→ˣ MUST HABIT BRUSH TEETH

Chapter Summary

In this chapter, you learned the following:

1. Vocabulary for medical personnel and the locations where they work.
2. Vocabulary and expressions to describe physical ailments.
3. Vocabulary for medical terminology.
4. Vocabulary for body parts.

QUIZ

All the sentences used in this quiz can be viewed on the DVD. You will need to view the sentences being signed in order to answer the questions.

1. What did the signer explain?
2. Where did the signer take her son?
3. What happened to the signer's friend?
4. With what type of doctor did the man make an appointment?
5. The signer described her ailments to the doctor. What were they?
6. Where is the signer's grandmother?
7. What does the signer need to do?
8. What did the signer do this morning?
9. What does the signer do every night?
10. To what medicine is the signer allergic?

APPENDIX
Glossing Conventions

1. A single capitalized English word is used to identify a single ASL sign.

HOUSE

2. Capitalized English words separated by hyphens represent a single ASL sign.

OH-I-SEE

3. Two capitalized English words connected by a ^ symbol indicate that two ASL signs have been combined into a single sign.

TRUE^BUSINESS

4. Capitalized letters separated by hyphens represent a sequence of alphabetic character signs used to spell a word.

S-H-E-L-F

5. A capitalized English word that begins with a # symbol represents a lexical ASL sign that originally began as a sequence of alphabetic character signs.

#JOB

6. PRO-1 is used to represent a first person singular pronoun. ASL does not have separate signs meaning "me" and "I" as English does.

PRO-1

7. Two capitalized English words within brackets represent two bound ASL morphemes.

{FOUR}{O'CLOCK}

8. A capitalized English word with a grammatical process in brackets next to it is used to gloss a sign that is modified.

STUDY[CONTINUATIVE]

9. When a sequence of glosses is accompanied by a nonmanual signal that provides a specific piece of grammatical information, a line is drawn over the glosses, which are followed by a symbol indicating the nonmanual sign that was expressed. Example: PRO-1 UNDERSTAND.

I don't understand.

10. When a gesture is used, its meaning within the specific context appears in quotation marks.

"don't know"

11. If a signer uses both hands at the same time to produce two different signs, the glosses are written on top of each other, the top line referring to the strong hand and the bottom line to the weak hand.

BOY
GIRL

12. ASL has a prefix that means "age of living thing." It attaches to numeral signs and is used to express age. This prefix is glossed as $\{AGE_0\}$.

13. There is a suffix in ASL that is glossed –ER and adds the meaning of "agent nominalizer" to verbs. It is produced by two B handshapes with the palms facing one another about shoulder-width apart and moving down from about the signer's shoulders to the trunk.

14. PRO$^{\rightarrow x}$ This indicates that the sign is directed toward entity x. Entity x will either be something (such as another person) in the signer's environment or an entity (like the "boy" and "girl" from our GIVE example) associated with that space.

15. |girl| The word enclosed in vertical brackets indicates the entity being identified.

16. GIVE$^{\rightarrow|girl|}$ The $^{\rightarrow|girl|}$ indicates that the sign is directed towards the area associated with |girl|.

17. GIVE$^{x\rightarrow y}$ The $^{x\rightarrow y}$ indicates that the sign begins nearer to and/or is directed toward x and then moves toward y, where entity y is either something (such as another person) in the signer's environment or an entity associated with that space.

18. GIVE$^{x\leftarrow y}$ The $^{x\leftarrow y}$ indicates that the sign begins nearer to and/or is directed toward y, then moves toward x.

19. INVITE$^{\leftarrow y}$ The $^{\leftarrow y}$ indicates that the verb begins directed toward y and then moves away from y.

20. GO$^{\rightarrow}$ The sign points in the direction of the action.

21. INFORM $^{[\text{RECIP}]X \leftrightarrow Y}$ This indicates that the hands move in opposite directions between x and y. In this sign, each hand produces only a single movement. In producing a one-handed sign such as SAME-DUAL$^{X \leftrightarrow Y}$, the hand moves back and forth between x and y.

22. PRO-PL$^{\supset a,b,c}$ The $^{\supset a,b,c}$ indicates that the hand moves along a path so that the extent of the path points toward entities a, b, and c.

23. SAY-NO-TO$^{\cup X}$ The $^{\cup X}$ indicates that the head and eyes are directed toward entity x.

24. HONOR$^{\cup \rightarrow y}$ The $^{\cup \rightarrow y}$ indicates that the face and eyes ($\cup$), as well as the hands ($\rightarrow$), are directed toward y.

25. MOVE $^{L1 \rightarrow L2}$ The $^{L1 \rightarrow L2}$ indicates that the hand begins directed toward location 1 and ends directed toward location 2.

26. THROW$^{\rightarrow L}$ The sign is directed toward location L.

ANSWER KEY TO CHAPTER QUIZZES

CHAPTER 1

1. False   2. False   3. False   4. False   5. 1817   6. William Stokoe   7. An international conference of deaf educators in Milan that decided the oral method should be used in educating deaf children rather than the manual method.   8. English words used to represent signs.   9. Handshape, location, and movement   10. 1965

CHAPTER 2

1. True   2. False   3. True   4. True   5. True   6. False   7. True   8. False   9. True
10. False

CHAPTER 3

1. True   2. a. B   b. V   c. H   3. a. O   b. ∪   c. ∩   4. a. ^   b. ⊥   c. •   5. True
6. True   7. False   8. True   9. False   10. True

CHAPTER 4

1. True   2. a, c, and e   3. False   4. a, d, and e   5. True   6. True   7. False
8. True   9. True   10. b, e, and f

CHAPTER 5

1. False   2. True   3. False   4. True   5. True   6. False   7. True   8. True
9. False   10. False

CHAPTER 6

1. Variation   2. Lexical   3. Dialect   4. True   5. True   6. False   7. True   8. False
9. True   10. False

CHAPTER 7

1. What is your name?   2. Nice to meet you.   3. Good/fine. OK.   4. Where do you live?   5. PRO-1 LIVE [name of state]   6. Are you deaf or hearing?   7. PRO-1 HEAR-

ING or DEAF   8. How long have you been studying ASL?   9. What is your job? What do you do?   10. PRO-1 [your profession].

CHAPTER 8

1. Yes/no   2. WH- question   3. Yes/no   4. Question mark wiggle   5. Rhetorical
6. YES or NO   7. When   8. Where   9. How   10. Which

CHAPTER 9

1. White and gray   2. Light blue   3. Soft   4. Tall   5. Short and thin   6. Shape
7. Square   8. Under the table   9. Under/near the window   10. Blond

CHAPTER 10

1. Like   2. No   3. Delicious   4. It was lousy.   5. It is old and dirty.   6. Yes
7. Won   8. Strange   9. Do you like the color green?   10. No

CHAPTER 11

1. Future   2. Past   3. Present   4. Future   5. Last week   6. Tomorrow   7. Next week   8. Now   9. Two days ago   10. Last week

CHAPTER 12

1. Careful finger spelling   2. Lexicalized sign   3. Lexicalized sign   4. Careful finger spelling   5. Careful finger spelling   6. Sarah   7. Texas   8. High school
9. Apartment   10. Television

CHAPTER 13

1. 173   2. Two   3. Sixteen   4. 42,893   5. Third   6. Fifty-nine   7. Monday, Wednesday, Friday   8. 6:00 A.M.   9. September   10. Eighteen dollars

CHAPTER 14

1. Four brothers, one sister   2. Two children   3. Her aunt's   4. The woman is pregnant.   5. Volleyball, basketball, and tennis   6. Seven years   7. Married   8. Eight
9. She flirted with a man.   10. Easter

CHAPTER 15

1. My son is sick.   2. To the emergency room   3. She fell and broke her arm.   4. Cardiologist   5. She is hot, tired, and having trouble breathing.   6. Intensive care unit
7. She needs to go to the bathroom.   8. She woke up, worked out, and then took a shower.   9. Brush her teeth   10. Penicillin

CHAPTER 16 (ON DVD)

1. She is going next week to visit her mom.   2. She bought an airplane ticket.   3. She flew to France last year.   4. One hour and 15 minutes due to heavy traffic.   5. Museum   6. Her favorite country is Spain because it has the best cuisine.   7. Walk four blocks and then turn right.   8. It was a beautiful country with bright green mountains and a blue ocean.   9. Her vacation was canceled because a snowstorm hit and caused the airport to close.   10. Spring

CHAPTER 17 (ON DVD)

1. She wants to eat now because she is starving.   2. She ate a lot and now is full.   3. Her daughter eats cereal for breakfast.   4. Her friend cooked dinner. The friend made spaghetti and salad.   5. Cheeseburger, French fries and a pop.   6. Apple, bananas, strawberry, and grapes   7. Peas, carrots, onions   8. She is eating sushi for lunch and needs chopsticks.   9. Mayonnaise and salt   10. She wants to order cheese pizza.

CHAPTER 18 (ON DVD)

1. She wants a new dress.   2. How much are these shoes?   3. She is going to an ATM machine because she needs more money.   4. Her sister exchanged her shirt because it was to large.   5. She is owed 50 dollars.   6. If you use a credit card, have identification ready.   7. She needs new glasses because her glasses broke.   8. She wore a red dress, black high heel shoes and had a white bag.   9. What size are you?   10. She prefers to shop online.

CHAPTER 19 (ON DVD)

1. She has a Mac.   2. The equipment needs new batteries.   3. Her phone number which is 721-9635.   4. She ordered new CDs.   5. Do you like video games?   6. Her internet connection is slow.   7. She needs forty copies.   8. Yesterday, she bought a new camera.   9. She needs to upgrade her software.   10. What is your email address?

CHAPTER 20 (ON DVD)

1. Are you learning ASL?   2. Do you enjoy school?   3. She failed the test she took last week.   4. To please pay attention.   5. She goes to the movies every once in a while.   6. Her friend teased her.   7. Who will be the next President? That is the big question.   8. Do you understand me?   9. She worked all night.   10. The boy is mischievous.

FINAL EXAM (ON DVD)

1. False   2. False.   3. True   4. True   5. True   6. True   7. (a) Plain (b) Indicating (c) Depicting   8. False. Depicting verbs do this.   9. False   10. True   11. False   12. True   13. True   14. True   15. False   16. True   17. True   18. False   19. False   20. True   21. False   22. False   23. True   24. True   25. Kim   26. Boston, MA   27. Washington, DC   28. Deaf   29. Deaf   30. Lawyer   31. Six years   32. Yes   33. No   34. Car accident   35. Three weeks ago Thursday   36. Left   37. Driver's side door   38. A broken left arm and broken ribs   39. Two   40. Orthopedist

INDEX

Accent, 100
Actions, 28–29
Age, 226–27
Age of acquisition, 109
Ago, expressing, 189
Alphabets
  consonant, 6
  manual, 203–14
  phonemic, 6
  syllabic, 6
American School for the Deaf, 3
American Sign Language (ASL)
  age of acquisition, 109
  historical change, 109–10
  history of, 2–6
  as a language, 1, 5
  lexicon, 81–82
  modality, 1
  morphology, 37–40 (*See also*
      Morphology)
  phonology, 32–37 (*See also*
      Phonology)
  pronouns, 41–46 (*See also*
      Pronouns)
  simultaneity, 2
  syntax, 50–60 (*See also* Syntax)
  variations, 99–112
      lexical, 103–4, 107
      phonological, 101–3, 107
      syntactic, 104–5
  verbs, 62–84 (*See also* Verbs)
  visual aspect, 1–2
Arabic system of writing, 6
Articulators, 22. *See also* Body as
      articulator; Facial expressions;
      Hand as articulator
  interaction of, 22, 50
ASL manual alphabet, 203–5. *See also*
      Finger spelling
Aspect, 18–19, 48–50
  definition, 48
  facial expressions, 50
  reduplication, 48–50

Body as articulator, 22–29
  actions, 28–29
  character, demonstrating a, 29
  discursive information, 23–27
      signers, 23–24
      topics, 24–27
  producing signs, 22
Body parts, 274–76

Braidwood system, 3
British manual alphabet, 203. *See also* Finger spelling
British Sign Language, 3
Burmese alphabet, 6

Casterline, Dorothy, 5
Character, conveying a, 21–22
Character, demonstrating reactions of a, 29
Chinese, 6
    Cantonese *vs.* Mandarin, 7
Citation form of verbs, 67–68, 82
Cities, signs for, 120–21
Clerc, Laurent, 3
Cogswell, Alice, 2
Cogswell, Mason Fitch, 3
Colors, 153–56
Commands, 53–54
Congregational Church of New England, 3
Conventions. *See* Glossing conventions; Signing space conventions
Conversational etiquette, 92–95
    physical descriptions, 96–97
Croneberg, Carl, 5
Cued speech, 14

Dates, 229–35
Days of week, 232–33
Deaf, The
    as cultural group, 85–86
    isolation, 3
    label of *deaf*, 85–86
    statistics, 3
Deaf etiquette, 85–98
    conversational etiquette, 92–95
    eye contact, 91
    getting attention, 89–90
    introductions, 86–88
    personal space, 91–92
    physical descriptions, 96–97
    sight lines, 90–91

Deaf *vs.* hearing, signs for, 122–25
Declarative statements, 51
Denison, James, 4
Departing, signs for, 132–33
Descriptions, 153–69
    colors, 153–56
    combining, 165–69
    positioning, 161–64
    shapes, 159–60
    sizes, 153–59
    surfaces, 153–59
    textures, 153–59
Dialects, 6, 100
Dictionary of American Sign Language on Linguistic Principles, A (Stokoe), 5
Direction of movement, 75
Discursive information, 20–21, 23–27

Emotive expression, 19–20
English
    lexicon, 81–82
Ethnic considerations, 107
Evaluative signs, 175–77
Eye gaze, 20–21, 91

Facial expressions
    aspect, 50
    conveying a character, 21–22
    discursive information, 20–21
    emotive *vs.* grammatical information, 16, 19–20
    verb aspect, 18–19
    voice intonation and, 17
Family, 241–48
Film, 7
Finger spelling, 203–14
    ASL manual alphabet, 203–5
    careful finger spelling, 203, 205–6
    comprehension, 206
    hand use, 203–4

lexicalized signs, 203, 206–13
  rapid finger spelling, 203
  uses of, 203
French Institute for the Deaf, 3
French Sign Language (LSF), 13
Friends, 248–52
Future, expressing, 194–99

Gallaudet, Edward Miner, 4, 5
Gallaudet, Thomas Hopkins, 2, 4
Gallaudet College, 4
  sign as language of instruction, 5
Gallaudet University, 4
  linguistics department, 35
Gender considerations, 108–9
Geographic regions, 107
Glossing conventions, 8–13, 285–87
  articulation, 11
  both hands, 12
  brackets, 11
  capital letters, 8, 9
  compounds, 8
  facial expressions, 18
  gesture, 12
  glosses on top of each other, 12
  hyphens, 8, 10
  morphemes, 11
  nonmanual signal, 12
  omissions, 9
  PRO-1, 11
  questions, 18, 51
  sign #, 10
  sign ^, 8, 10
  spelling, 10
Good-bye, signs for, 132–33
Grammar structure, 32–61. *See also*
      Specific grammatical topics
  vs. concept, 2
Great Plains Indians, 2–6
Greek alphabet, 6
Greetings, signs for, 113–32

Hand as articulator, 12, 22
  orientation, 102–3
Hartford, Connecticut, 2
Health
  body parts, 274–76
  describing, 117–18, 262–70
  forming sentences, 280–82
  medical professions, 259–62
  medical terminology, 270–74
  miscellaneous vocabulary, 277–79
Hearing *vs.* deaf, signs for, 122–25
Henniker, New Hampshire community, 3
Historical change of language, 109–10
Holidays, 253–55

Introductions, 86–88
  signs for, 113–32

Japanese, 6
Johnson, Robert E., 35–37

Kendall, Amos, 4

Lambert, Jonathan, 3
Language
  vs. speech, 6
Language variation, 99–112
  age of acquisition, 109
  definition, 99–100
  historical change of language, 109–10
  linguistic reasons for, 105–7
  social reasons for, 107–9
  types of variation, 99–105
Lexicon, 81–82
  lexical variation, 99–100
Liddell, Scott K., 35–37
Likes and dislikes, 170–86
  concepts, 177–79
  evaluative signs, 175–77
  preferences, 171–75
  signing sentences, 180–85

Linguistics of Visual English, 14
Lip-reading, 5, 95–96
Location, signing, 69–70, 75, 101–3,
    161–64. *See also* Space, signing
Logographic system of writing, 6

Malay, 47
Marriage, signs for, 131
Martha's Vineyard community,
    3–4
Martha's Vineyard Sign Language
    (MVSL), 4
Massieu, Jean, 3
Medicine. *See* Health
Meetings. *See* Introductions
Metathesis, 102
Milan international conference, 4
Money, 227–29
Months, 234–35
Morphology, 37–40
    bound morphemes, 38
    definition, 37–38
    free morphemes, 38
    prefixes, 38–40
    restrictions, 39
    suffixes, 38–40

Names, signs for, 114–16
National Association of the Deaf
    (NAD), 5
    preserving ASL, 7
Negation, 52
New York School for the Deaf, 4
Nonmanual signal (NMS), 50–54
Nose gestures, 20
Numbers
    age, 226–27
    cardinal, 215–24
    dates, 229–35
    money, 227–29
    ordinal, 224–26

Oral education, 4–5
Orientation of hand, 102–3

Parenthood, signs for, 132
Past, expressing, 187–93
Peet, Isaac, 4
Pennsylvania School for the Deaf, 4
Personal space, 91–92
Phonology, 32–37
    definition, 32
    handshape, 33
    location, 33
    movement, 33
    phonology of signs, 33–35
    postures, 37
    sequence of segments, 36–37
    symbols of parts, 33–35
    transitions, 37
    variation, 101–3, 107
Physical descriptions, 96–97
Placement, 102
Positioning, 161–64
Postures, 37
Preferences, 171–75. *See also* Likes and
    dislikes
Prefix, 38–40
    age of living thing, 38
Present, expressing, 193–94
Preservation of the Sign Language,
    7
Pronouns, 41–46
    definition, 41
    first person *vs.* non-first person,
        41–43
    number, 41, 43–45

Question mark wiggle, 150
Questions, 51–52, 135–52
    rhetorical, 148–50
    WH-, 138–48
    yes/no, 135–38

Quizzes
  answers, 288–89
  body as articulator, 30–31
  descriptions, 168–69
  family and friends, 258
  finger spelling, 214
  grammar structure, 61
  greetings and good-byes, 134
  health, 283
  introduction, 15
  likes and dislikes, 186
  numbers, 239–40
  questions, 151–52
  time, 202
  variation, 111–12
  verbs, 83–84

Reduplication, 47–50
  aspect, 48–50
  time, 47–48
Relationships
  family, 241–48
  friends, 248–52
Rhetorical questions, 148–50

School, signs for, 125–27, 129–30
Schools for deaf, 2
Sentence structure, 50–61
Shapes, 159–60
Sicard, Abb{e acu}, 3
Sight lines, 90–91
Sign communication systems, 13–14
Sign Language Structure: An Outline of the Visual Communication System of the American Deaf (Stokoe), 5
Sign languages
  around the world, 13
  preserving, 7
Signers, indicating, 23–24
Signing Exact English 1, 14
Signing Exact English 2, 14

Signing space conventions, 70
SignWriting, 7
Simultaneous communication (Sim-Com), 14
Sizes, 153–59
Space, signing, 68
  location, 69–70
  signing space conventions, 70
  tokens, 68
Spatial timeline, 201
Sports, 255–57
States, signs for, 120–21
Stoddard, Charles, 4
Stokoe, William C., 5–6
  phonology of signs, 33–35
Stokoe Notation System, 7
Storytelling tradition, 7
Suffix, 38–40
  -er, 39–40
Surfaces, 153–59
Sutton, Valerie, 7
Syllabaries, 6
Syntax, 50–60
  commands, 53–54
  declarative statements, 51
  negation, 52
  nonmanual signal (NMS), 50–54
  questions, 51–52
  topics, marking, 52–53
  word order, 54–60 (*See also* Word order)
Syntax variation, 100

Textures, 153–59
Time
  changing tense, 199–200
  expressing future, 194–99
  expressing past, 187–93
  expressing present, 193–94
  reduplication, 47–48
  spatial timeline, 201
  telling time, 235–39

Tokens, 68
Tomorrow, expressing, 195, 197
Topics, indicating, 24–27
Topics, marking, 52–53
Transitions, 37

Veditz, George W., 7
Verbs, 62–84
    aspect, 18–19
    changing tense, 199–200
        (*See also* Time)
    citation form of verbs, 67–68
    depicting, 76–83
        arrangement of entities,
            80
        BE-AT, 77–78
        movement of action,
            80–81
        shape and extent of surface,
            78–80

indicating, 67–76
        list, 71–73
    inflection, 62
    plain, 63–67
    reciprocal, 73–75
    tense (*See* Time)

WH- questions, 138–48
Word order
    (SVO), 54–55
    (SVPRO-Copy), 58–59
    (TSV), 58
    (TVO), 57
    (VO), 55–57
    (VPRO-Copy), 59–60
Work, signs for, 127–28
Written language, 6, 7
    as artificial, 7

Yes/no questions, 135–38